THE CATSKILLS
A Winter Sports Guide

THE CATSKILLS
A Winter Sports Guide

by

GEORGE V. QUINN

PURPLE MOUNTAIN PRESS

Fleischmanns, New York

Dedication

In memory of my mother, Hilde, whose encouragement made this book possible.

The Catskills: A Winter Sports Guide
First edition 2001

Much of the material in this book appeared first in *The Catskills: A Cross-Country Skiing Guide* by George V. Quinn (Purple Mountain Press, 1997).

Published by PURPLE MOUNTAIN PRESS, LTD.
1060 Main Street, P.O. Box 309, Fleischmanns, New York 12430-0309
845-254-4062 845-254-4476 (fax) purple@catskill.net
http://www.catskill.net/purple

Library of Congress Control Number: 2001 135763
International Standard Book Number: 1-930098-28-6
Manufactured in the United States of America on acid-free paper.

Caution

Outdoor recreation activities are by their very nature potentially hazardous and contain risk. All participants in such activities must assume responsibility for their own actions and safety. The outdoors are forever changing. No book can replace good judgment. The author and the publisher cannot be held responsible for inaccuracies, errors, or omissions or for changes in the details in this publication or for the consequences of any reliance on the information contained herein or for the safety of people in the outdoors.

Table of Contents

Map Legends

--- SKI TRAIL   ④ COUNTY ROAD

•••• HIKING TRAIL   ▲ MOUNTAIN

[P] PARKING   ♠ LEAN - TO

✦ LOOK OUT   Y TRAIL MARKER

㉘ STATE ROAD   ✳ WATERFALL

⋈ BRIDGE   ≋ STEEP AREA (caution)

Introduction

The past winter was extraordinary: long, cold, snowy; a winter that comes around every 10 years or so. Some called it *2001: A Snow Odyssey*.

As I write, it is April, and there is still a dense snowpack on many of the north-facing mountainsides. Winter sports enthusiasts are still skiing and snow-shoeing on backcountry trails, so I decided to do Slide Mountain. At the trailhead I could barely get in the parking area due to the high mounds of snow. The snow depth in the woods on Slide was at least four feet or more; ideal for woods skiing as most hazards and obstacles were well buried beneath the snow-pack. Several others with telemark skis and snow-boards were there to climb the mountain. They included a group of four extreme skiers planning to ski the treacherous slide below the summit that gives the mountain its name.

The initial climb was routine enough, but higher the icing on trees became so intense branches sagged in our faces, and on this bright sunny day in early April on the south side, we found ourselves in a bar-rage of ice crystals and frigid water. My worn fleece jacket, gloves and backpack were soon soaked. As I maneuvered around to the top north ridge using my climbing skins, any semblance of a trail disappeared. The ice, up to two feet thick, collapsed durable bal-sams and hardwoods on the trail making it impenetra-ble. The ascent now became a bushwhack following wherever the footprints I could find along the top ridge. State trail markers (at feet level) came into view for the last push for the summit.

I caught up with the extreme skiers on the very summit of the mountain. They had just started to de-scend the steep north face by foot with the help of poles to stay on top of the snowpack. We inched our way through thick, stunted balsam trees searching for the top of the great slide. I was behind them ready to take some photographs. It was extremely slow going. The eight feet or more of snowpack on the Catskills' highest elevation became hard to walk on. The underlying terrain was riddled with shafts and ledges; one could disappear in the snow at any time. After taking pictures above the ravine that drops 3,000 feet, I decided to turn back. I was still soaked, and it was well below freezing in the shade. After yelling goodbye and good luck to the others, I turned toward the nearly vertical pitch of the mountain, took my first step, and immediately sank up to my waist. After grabbing a branch to pull myself up, I sank even deeper on my second try. I was now mired and wondered who would ever find me here way off the trail in the snow-muffled silence. Perhaps Jerimiah Johnson. Trying to keep my wits, I realized that by using my shins and knees like snowshoes and with my arms spread out, I could stay on top of the snow. It was a very slow crawl back to the summit, but I was motivated by the scant rays of sun visible ahead through the dark forest. Reaching them, I could defrost and dry out.

After attaining the Burroughs Rock and summit lookout, I was too exhausted to fully appreciate the view. I knew it was a hellish ski-hike down the top ridge, nearly three miles and a 1,600' vertical drop back to the trailhead. It was now getting late in the day.

A stiff northwest wind had picked up adding to the chill of my wet clothing. It wasn't until I reached the south side that spring returned, and the snow was soft enough to ski with room enough to make telemark turns. As for the extreme skiers, I have not read in the newspaper that they are missing.

I hope you will never encounter a situation like my Slide Mountain adventure. Nordic skiing is generally safer than the downhill variety. My concern is for everyone using this guide to have a safe return. Remember that trails and areas change over time, either by official designation or by forces of nature. I have tried to be as accurate as possible. If you feel any descriptions are vague or unclear, please feel free to write me:

George V. Quinn
P.O. Box 141
Boiceville NY 12412

See you on the trail.

A Brief History of Skiing in the Catskills

Looking out over the Catskills, one sees an expanse of mountains and ridges with deep valleys between. The tops of these mountains extend for miles at over 3,000 feet in elevation, which is unusual in the Northeast.

The Catskills are relatively old geologically. During the Devonian Period, approximately 400 to 350 million years ago, the area was below a shallow ocean. Thousands of feet of sediment accumulated from the runoff of newly created mountains, and eventually formed the Catskill Delta. Sedimentary rock was formed by the forces of nature working in the shallow sea covering the region. Sometime during this period, the whole region uplifted rather than buckled, forming the Catskill Plateau. The hard conglomerate cap eroded in places, making deep valleys and canyons wherever it wore through; Kaaterskill and Plattekill Cloves on the eastern escarpment are dramatic examples of this process.

The Ice Ages of 2 million to 10,000 years ago further sculpted the land and left the Catskills with 98 mountains over 3,000 feet high. It was inevitable that this topography would entice skiers in the twentieth century.

Scandinavian immigrants—the descendants of people who skied for many centuries—brought their skis with them, or fashioned new ones consisting of a length of ash or hickory, with a curved and carved tip and a single leather strap holding the foot in place. Local farmers improvised with barrel staves, which made for winter fun sliding around the farm. Some of these first cross-country skis are on display at the Hunter Mountain Lodge.

Along the trail in the early 1940s.

During the 1920s, downhill skiing slowly came to national recognition, although it mainly consisted of hiking up a small hill and gliding down. A ski run was started on a farm near Climax, in Greene County, in the 1920s, and several hundred people came out on weekends to try out the new sport. The big ski boom started when the 1932 Winter Olympics at Lake Placid in the northern Adirondacks introduced both downhill and cross-country ski events to the United States.

The differing attractions of alpine and nordic skiing became apparent early on. The *Mount Mansfield* (Vermont) *Bulletin* reported in 1940, "We cannot but feel that the proponents of cross-country skiing are wasting their time trying to popularize it. Some things just have not got what it takes to be universally popular, and ski touring is one of them. Touring requires imagination and an appreciation of solitude, which the majority of people do no have or do not want."

In the mid-1930s, Phoenicia, in Ulster County, became the focus of the ski craze with the building of the Simpson Ski Slope on a small mountain next to the train tracks above the Esopus Creek. With the help of the Civilian Conservation Corps, several wide slopes and rope tows were constructed. Ski trains began running weekend specials and hordes of skiers descended on Phoenicia, filling the few hotels and lodging houses. The original lodge is still standing, though the slope closed in the early seventies and is now returning to forest.

Some towns, sensing the financial potential of skiing, built small slopes and added toboggan runs. In Rosendale, also in Ulster County, a large ski jump was constructed in the late 1930s and drew substantial crowds for many years. A lull occurred during World War II, but interest in the sport resumed after the war ended. When troops of the Tenth Mountain Division, trained in ski mountaineering, returned from the war, they were instrumental in the growth of the ski industry in the Catskills and nationwide.

The Davenport family opened Highmount Ski Center on Belleayre Mountain in 1946. After voters approved a referendum to allow a ski center in the constitutionally-protected forest preserve, a lodge and trail system were constructed by the state just east of Highmount. When Belleayre Mountain Ski Center opened in 1948 it offered a single chairlift and some rather treacherous rope tows. By the 1950s, more ski areas had been developed, bringing increased ski traffic from metropolitan New York City. Some areas were quite primitive, with rural entrepreneurs installing small T-bars or rope tows on backyard hillsides and charging a fee to help ends meet during the long, cold Catskill winters. Liability costs were not a major concern at the time.

Large areas also were developed. At the Princeton Ski Bowl near Prattsville, which reached to 3,600 feet, skiers took specially outfitted buses up long, winding roads to the summit. Several very snowy winters in the 1950s fostered more construction, some of it foolish—several areas were built on southern exposures that had little chance of surviving a mild winter. At one time there were more than a dozen downhill areas operating in the Catskills. At the time of this writing, there are only seven left. High liability insurance, infrastructure improvement costs, and increased competition from other areas have taken their toll.

Cross-country skiing increased in popularity during the 1970s with the advent of waxless skis, which meant one could go out skiing without the hassle of waxing. Belleayre Mountain Ski Center, owned and operated by the New York State Department of Environmental Conservation (DEC), was one of the first to start a trail system for nordic skiers, and others, seeing the potential, have followed. Several private touring centers have been laid out just for nordic skiing and offer extensive trail systems.

Some of the best skiing is within the forest preserve, which was created in 1885. The Catskill Park was established in 1904 and includes parts of Delaware, Greene, Sullivan, and Ulster Counties, where some state-owned land has been constituted "forever wild." The park is a checkerboard of public and private lands. The preserve grew to 280,000 acres by the mid-1980s and still is expanding through gifts and purchases.

Much has been done in the last decade to ensure access to landlocked state lands through right-of-way purchases. Some forest preserve trails are designated for nordic skiing, and are marked for that purpose. Today there are many places to ski and snowshoe, and the popularity of the sports has grown immensely.

Trails that are especially suitable for nordic skiing are those that follow old wagon or logging roads. Also very skiable are old carriage roads leading to the sites of defunct mountaintop hotels, and jeep roads leading to fire tower sites. Several roads, now abandoned, rise between the notches of the highest peaks. Before the automobile, they were the quickest way to move goods from valley to valley. Today they offer fine views for the cross-country skier.

Catskill Mountain Weather

Knowledge of weather patterns will help in planning extended outings in the higher Catskill terrain. Some state-marked trails reach several miles into the back country and up to the highest peaks, where temperatures and precipitation may vary drastically from that in the valleys below. Many of the trails in this book are located at least 2,000 feet high. Snows may come as early as late September and as late as May to mountains above 3,000 feet. Wind chill must be considered carefully when planning to go up the higher peaks, as winds there may reach hurricane strength in some snowstorms.

Weather reports generally come from National Weather Service at Poughkeepsie, Kingston or Albany—located near sea level. Generally a rise of a thousand feet means a temperature drop of approximately three degrees. Wind direction also plays an important role in mountain weather patterns. Winds from the south or southeast may bring warmer weather and more uniform temperatures at different elevations; winds from the east or northeast usually bring moisture off the Atlantic Ocean and snow to higher elevations.

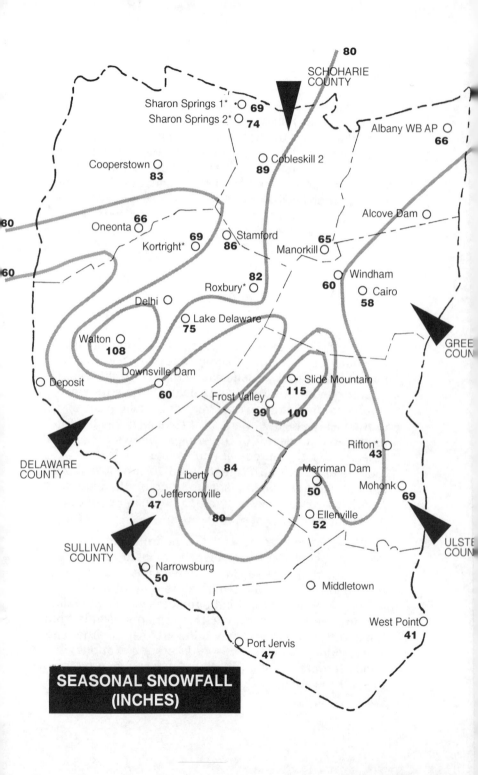

80

SCHOHARIE
COUNTY

Sharon Springs 1* ○ **69**
Sharon Springs 2* ○ **74**

Albany WB AP ○
66

Cooperstown ○
83

○ Cobleskill 2
89

Alcove Dam ○

80

○ **66**
Oneonta ○

Kortright* ○ **69**

○ Stamford
86

Manorkill ○ **65**

60

Delhi ○

Roxbury* ○ **82**

○ Windham
60

○ Cairo
58

○ Lake Delaware
75

Walton ○
108

Downsville Dam ○

○ Deposit

60

○ Slide Mountain
115

Frost Valley
99   **100**

Rifton* ○
43

GREE
COUN

DELAWARE
COUNTY

Liberty ○ **84**

Merriman Dam
○
50

Mohonk ○
69

○ Jeffersonville
47

80

○ Ellenville
52

SULLIVAN
COUNTY

○ Narrowsburg
50

○ Middletown

ULSTE
COUN

West Point ○
41

○ Port Jervis
47

**SEASONAL SNOWFALL
(INCHES)**

A major difference occurs when the wind comes from the north, northwest or west. Colder air then has to rise over the higher ridges, and moisture-laden winds condense, forming snow over the high Catskills. The air expands and warms when dipping into the Hudson Valley in an effect known as "downsloping." This phenomenon is very pronounced in March and April, when temperature differences are the greatest. It is not uncommon to find snow at Belleayre Mountain any day in March, while in Kingston, 30 miles to the southeast, it may be a pleasant spring day with sunshine and temperatures in the 50s.

Seasonal snowfall totals through the years indicate that the greatest accumulations are over the Slide Mountain area, with an average of more than 115 inches recorded yearly at the weather station, located at 2,650 feet. Several more feet surely must fall at the 4,180-foot summit, where there is no permanent weather station. A snowbelt extends south from Slide, with lessening amounts toward the village of Liberty. This area encompasses many of the highest peaks and the higher valleys, such as Frost Valley and Denning. Notably, the Walton area in the western Catskills receives an average of 108 inches of snowfall, though it does not have nearly the elevation of the Slide Mountain region. The Walton area is closer to the lake-effect snow of Lake Ontario, and it receives many snows that do not reach the eastern Catskills. Like other mountain ranges, some years the snows favor certain areas over others.

To summarize: Catskill winters are unreliable, so it's best to check all the corners of the region for winter activities.

Opposite page: Chart from *Catskill Weather* by Jerome Thaler (Purple Mountain Press, 1996).

Winter Travel

Areas such as Belleayre Mountain Ski Center and Wilson State Park are usually accessible during periods of prolonged snow, but traveling off the main roads requires careful planning in inclement weather. Areas such as Slide Mountain, Diamond Notch and Adler Lake are remote and high in the mountains, and offer no amenities.

Items to bring along in your car for emergencies include a snow shovel, battery jumper cables, a flashlight, tow rope, de-icer for door locks, extra clothing, food and water. A full tank of gas is a good idea. Park your car facing out in case you need a battery jump. Use common sense in hiding your valuables. Keys should be zipped in an inner parka or vest pocket. Keep your vehicle well maintained. In snowy conditions, travel in high mountain areas with steep access roads, such as Slide or Balsam Lake Mountains, requires front-wheel—if not four-wheel—drive with good tire tread. Bringing the telephone number of a service station or tow operator may not be a bad idea.

Parking

This book offers parking information for each trail covered to guide you in planning your trip. Many of the trailhead areas or DEC parking lots are plowed for winter access. However, some lots may not be plowed immediately after a snowstorm and may take considerable time to clear.

Always park your car in a safe or properly designated area. If parking along a state, county or town highway, find a space well off to the side. Snow plows must be able to circumnavigate your vehicle. If you can't get off the road properly, it might be necessary to shovel out a space. This may sound like hard work, but it could prevent an accident or unnecessary aggravation.

Snowmobile Trails

Only a few of the trails listed in this book are also used by snowmobilers. On forest preserve land, snowmobiles are allowed on designated trails only, and on frozen lakes and ponds where access may be gained by public roads onto marked snowmobile trails. Otherwise, snowmobiles are not permitted in the forest preserve.

There are several schools of thought when it comes to sharing snowmobile trails. Purists may want to avoid any trail where noisy machines detract from the wilderness experience. There are benefits, however, to skiing snowmobile trails. In deep, fresh snow, these trails may be easier to ski than unpacked trails, which may rapidly wear you out. In certain weather conditions, the snow on the packed trails may last longer than in the surrounding woods.

Use common sense when sharing a trail with snowmobilers. Although the rules say snowmobile drivers must yield the right-of-way to nordic skiers, standing beside the trail is wise when you meet or they pass. Extra caution is required when skiing in road cuts, winding trails and thick evergreens, where visibility is minimal. Most snowmobilers are out blazing trail on the weekends and evenings, so on weekdays you may discover that you have these trails to yourself.

Health and Safety

Cross-country skiing is rated as one of the best exercises for all-around muscle tone. At the recreational level, it burns off at least 500 calories an hour; it also relaxes the mind and relieves tension. Being out on a trail with only the whisper of the wind and the sound of your own breathing can be a spiritual experience. To enjoy the sport fully always use common sense and follow a few basic safety rules.

For starters, use trails that match your ability. Know your limits. If you are inexperienced, it is best always to ski with a friend or a group of people who can guide you along.

Skiing alone
For the more advanced skier, perhaps the best wilderness experience is skiing into the woods alone. It may offer the best chance to glimpse wildlife and experience the profound silence of the forest in winter. There is also a certain feeling of self-confidence that comes with mastering a challenge.

There are inherent dangers in going into the back country alone, including injuries, so it is wise to leave behind an exact itinerary with someone responsible. Almost all state trails have trail registers; signing in with your route and destination can help forest rangers locate you should the need arise.

Skiing with children
When skiing with children for the first time, make sure they are comfortable with the weather and the surroundings. The weather should be reasonably fair so as not to freeze fingers or toes. Start in the backyard or on an easy slope, because the youngster may want to stop at any time. The next step may be to visit a touring center where lessons are available, and where the child can watch other people skiing. If the child feels comfortable and has basic ability, it may be appropriate to go to the state trails and into more wilderness areas. Take it one step at a time.

Planning your trip
Planning the length of time your trip requires is very important. Trying to find the way back in a cold, dark winter night has caught many a nordic skier off guard. It is best to leave a lot of time for the return trip, especially in mid-winter, when darkness arrives on the northern or shaded sides of mountains as early as 4:30 P.M.

The length of time it takes to ski a trail depends on many factors: In deep, fresh snow you may travel at less than 1 mile per hour, whereas on a groomed, hard track, you could ski 5 miles or more in a hour.

Some kind of backpack is essential if skiing for more than an hour from a trailhead. The first thing to put in is an extra pair of dry socks. Other items include wooden matches, ace bandages, maps or trail guides, compass, heat packs, extra clothing, "space blanket," flashlight, knife, water, and high-energy bars or nuts and granola.

Ski components can be damaged. Common problems include binding screws that loosen, or skis that delaminate at the tip or the tail. Nordic shoes have been known to delaminate at the toes, which makes skiing nearly impossible. It is necessary to prepare for the worst, as many experienced skiers have found out the hard way. Bring along some nylon string or duct tape to keep delaminated layers together. A retractable-blade utility knife can come in handy for cutting off any parts of a ski that have sheered off and drag in the snow. Bring a posidrive screwdriver or one that is compatible with the system you are using to tighten any loose screws. The best preventive measure is to check your skis *before* every extended outing and make sure the screws are tight. If they are loose, remove them, fill the hole with epoxy, then gently tighten the screws again. If in doubt about the condition of your skis, take them to a ski shop for a visual inspection to determine if the screw holes are still good.

Hypothermia and other hazards

It is important in frigid weather to be aware of the danger of hypothermia, or lowered body temperature, in both yourself and your companions. Frostbite is also a danger when skiing on cold windy days. To acquaint yourself with these and other dangers and their prevention, we highly recommend a book published by the Adirondack Mountain Club called *Winterwise: A Backpacker's Guide* by John M. Dunn, M.D. It is a step-by-step tutorial on food, drink, clothing and shelter, and it can be used effectively by cross-country skiers, hikers, or campers. (See List of Useful Publications.)

Skiing on ice

It is generally recommended not to ski on a lake or pond unless you are very familiar with it. If unsure of ice conditions, ski gently over the ice with the bales of the binding open. A fragile mantle of snow may camouflage thin spots, and springs near the shores may keep the ice shallow, even in the coldest weather. Getting your skis wet means they will ice up and you will be unable to glide. If possible, dry them immediately before placing them back in the snow, or let the bottoms sit in the sunlight. A plastic ice scraper can prove invaluable.

Giardiasis

Something new at trailheads is the warning of giardiasis posted on the bulletin boards. Giardiasis is a disease caused by drinking contaminated water. Many a seemingly pristine water source may actually start at a contaminated source, such as a pond where the parasite is present even in the winter. Always carry plenty of your own water. More information can be obtained by reading the warnings on DEC posters displayed on the bulletin boards or by writing the DEC (see Appendix).

Clothing

Cross-country skiing uses all the major muscle groups in the body, and a good amount of heat (perspiration) is generated. When the sun comes out on a windless day, layers of clothes will soon come off. The first rule is to peel them off as soon as overheating begins. Wearing the proper clothing helps with this problem. Cotton, despite its natural, advertised qualities, is not a desirable fabric for cross-country skiing because it holds a lot of moisture and becomes cold when damp. Materials that are good at wicking away moisture are polypropylene, wool, and silk.

In very cold weather, polypropylene underwear and wool pants are recommended. Tops should be long enough to cover your lower back. Fleece jackets are excellent because of their low bulk but more protection might be needed in high wind-chill conditions, so bring along a sweater or parka.

Good leather gloves with Thinsulate™ insulation are best in cold weather. Mittens may give extra warmth, but they make grabbing the pole handles more difficult. Heat packs come in handy when the temperature drops in the late afternoon. Cross-country ski gloves are usually lighter than the downhill variety and have leather palms, but they may not be as warm.

Socks are very important for your nordic well being. It is best to wear a polypropylene liner under a thick wool or blended-fiber sock; bring an extra pair along on extended outings. Gaiters are essential when breaking new trail, as they prevent snow from getting in around the ankles.

A good knit cap is essential on cold windy days, but as soon as the temperature warms in the sun, a headband may suffice. The clothing needed to be prepared for different weather conditions is another reason to bring a backpack. Dr. Dunn's *Winterwise* is recommended on the subject of appropriate clothing.

Ski Equipment

There are several types of cross-country skis to choose from. Until the late 1960s, only wooden skis were available, but now technology has brought new synthetic materials that may enhance the nordic skiing experience.

Skis
For the recreational skier, a light-touring ski is fine. These skis are generally thin at the mid section and are good for most situations. Back-country skis are becoming more popular for extended trips in the wilder-

ness. They are wider and ride over deeper snow. Some may have metal edges for increased grip on hardpack. There is more camber, or bounce, in the ski to help initiate turns. Telemark skis are the next step up and are popular on downhill slopes as well as at cross-country areas. With a width of about 60 millimeters, they give maximum support for heavy use, or when carrying the additional weight of a loaded backpack; telemark boots are heavier and give more ankle support. Racing skis are very light and narrow; skating skis are used on wide, packed trails and have muted tips and no groove on the bottom.

When visiting a ski shop, explain exactly how well you ski and how much skiing you intend to do. Shop personnel usually fit skis by holding your hand straight up above your head and measuring the length in centimeters from the floor to your wrist. Other factors may affect the length, such as your weight, ability, and personal preferences.

Most cross-country skis sold today are waxless recreational skis, fine for most purposes. Anyone wanting to get the most out of nordic skiing may want to try waxing, especially in powder conditions where climbing and gliding can be enhanced by proper waxing.

There are several types of bindings to chose from. The three-pin, 75 millimeter toe binding has been popular for a long time and is compatible with many brand-name cross-country shoes. A heel locator or wedge is helpful for turning. Other binding systems, which may give better performance, are available—however, the binding and the boot must be compatible, which can make it impossible to "mix and match" boots and skis. It is best to have the bindings mounted by professionals (it is very easy to strip the screw holes).

Boots   Boots also come in many shapes and sizes. When trying on boots, be sure to wear a thick sock, or one that you will be wearing, in order to get the proper fit. Some movement in the toes is necessary to prevent cold feet, but your heel should not lift out of the boot. A boot that comes above the ankles with a cuff to keep out moisture also gives more stability, especially in turning.

Poles Poles come in many different styles as well. For the recreational skier, fiberglass poles are generally used because they are lightweight and economical, though they may break and splinter, so for back-country hikes it may be worth a few extra dollars to buy metal poles. The pole should reach armpit level. Recently, adjustable or telescopic poles have become popular and are used for racing.

Climbing skins Climbing skins are an especially useful nordic accessory. They attach to the bottoms of the skis for climbing steep inclines. These used to be made from sealskins, but now they are made of synthetic material. Because of the time involved in putting them on and taking them off, they are best used on longer hikes. Some skis come with strips of skin glued to the base of the ski and work quite well, although they are getting harder to find.

Telemark Equipment

The last decade has seen radical changes in telemark equipment. Skis that were once straight, narrow, and tall have now followed the trend in downhill skis to become shorter and more shaped with broader tips and tails that carve the snow better. Telemark ski equipment is a specialized item to shop for; not all ski shops carry or rent it. None of this equipment is cheap, therefore, look for an experienced salesperson to help you because there are many choices to be made.

Boots

Boots: There are so many choices to be made shopping for boots. If you ski frequently and are aggressive, you may want to spend the money and go for the top of the line. Just remember the three criteria for buying boots: fit, fit, and fit. Some boots will be heavier and stiffer and may be harder to use climbing a trail, however, you will get more performance from them on the way down.

Bindings

Bindings: Once telemark bindings were all cables of a front-throw variety but that has changed radically. Step-in bindings with brakes have arrived and have made it more convenient to get in and out with your boots. Hybrid-variety bindings now can accept either downhill or telemark boots. And, yes, they do make bindings that release. The weight of the binding must be considered for back-country travels: light is nice, but don't forget you have to come down that icy slope you just climbed.

Camping

Winter is a unique time to experience camping in the wilderness. State campsites and lean-tos are empty and bugs are virtually non-existent. State law prohibits camping in the fragile environment above 3,500 feet from March 22 to December 21, but because the snow pack acts as a buffer, camping is permitted at these higher elevations in mid-winter.

Survival gear is necessary when camping in the mountains because of potentially high wind-chill factors. New York State law requires that all campsites be located at least 150 feet from any water source.

Using This Guide

Each trail or ski-touring center in this book includes a description of the area, the trail (with elevation levels), the trail bases and suggested ability ratings. No estimated times are given due to the many factors than may alter one's speed.

Maps The maps show state-marked cross-country trails. A trail description without a map is for a private or state-run area which supplies its own maps. It is important to note that trail systems may change over time. The maps are intended to give an overview of the entire trail and the road area surrounding it. The text describes important topographical features and helps familiarize you with each trail. One-way mileage is listed for most trails unless otherwise stated. Do not back-country ski in wilderness areas without *good* maps, compass, etc. Even marked trails can be difficult to follow in winter.

Rating Your Ability

The following criteria have been established as a guide for rating the difficulty of each trail in this book. Remember, however, that snow conditions can change the rating of a trail. For example, a trail that is easy skiing for a beginner or novice under deep, fresh powder conditions may become dangerous and require expert skills when packed or icy, when it becomes much harder to stop or turn. Judge yourself and the trail accordingly.

Beginner
A *beginner* trail is suitable for a skier who has never skied or has had one or two lessons. It is limited to flat surfaces and/or slight inclines. A novice who goes beyond his or her backyard is advised to stick to groomed and patrolled areas and not to ski alone.

Intermediate
The *intermediate* designation is for the nordic skier who has considerable experience at stopping, knows basic turning maneuvers, has a basic knowledge of snow conditions and is able to judge properly his or her ability in relation to a trail. Stamina is important for trips of up to 10 miles. Proper preparation for adverse conditions and the ability to read a map are advisable.

Expert
The *expert* trail is only for the skier who has mastered all skills of turning and stopping and has a thorough knowledge of waxing skis. Moutaineering and survival skills, including the ability to read a compass, are required when skiing in the back country. The expert skier knows his or her endurance limit and acts accordingly.

1• Overlook Mountain

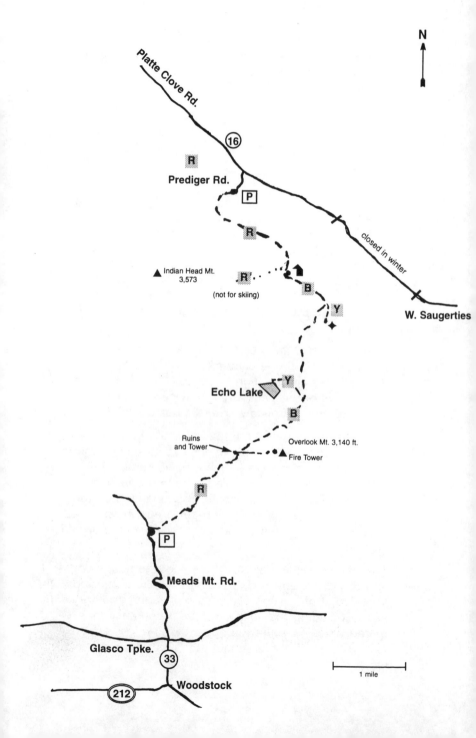

The Trails

Northern

1. OVERLOOK MOUNTAIN

Intermediate-Expert

Cross-Country Telemark Snowshoe

This nordic trail follows parts of an old wagon road, rich in history, from the top of Platte Clove (also known as Devil's Kitchen) to the summit of Overlook Mountain more than 6 miles away. The trail has little traffic in winter months and makes a splendid journey high along the escarpment to the fire tower on Overlook, at an elevation of 3,140 feet. There are few expert sections, but endurance and planning are important if one wants to take the long excursion to the top of Overlook Mountain. The approach from the Woodstock trailhead (Meads) is considerably shorter, but has much steeper grades that require expert skills. It may also be plowed.

The ruins of the Overlook Mountain House, whose origins date back to the 1870s are still present on the summit. There are excellent views in all direction from the recently restored fire tower.

Overlook Mountain House ruins captured in a Brownie-camera snapshot by the author in 1962.

Getting There At traffic light and NY Route 23A in Tannersville: Turn south on County Route 16. Bear right at 0.3 miles at Spring Street junction. At 1.3 miles bear left at Bloomer Road, staying on County 16 (now Platte Clove Road). At 5.7 miles make a right on Predigar Road and travel 0.4 miles farther to the parking area by a fence. Do not park by buildings. This is a town road and there is room for several cars. Note that Platte Clove Road from West Saugerties is closed in winter.

Alternate approach from Woodstock: From the village green in the center of town, go 0.6 miles north on Rock City Road (County Route 33) to junction of Glasco Turnpike. Proceed straight up Meads Mountain Road 2.1 miles to the height of the land, where there is a large parking area on right. The drive between trailheads in good weather is one hour.

The Trail From the parking area at the 2,000-foot level on Predigar Road, pass through opening in the fence and go across small creek; follow red trail markers to trail register at 0.1 miles. Yellow nordic ski-trail markers are also present. The trail follows easy grades for 0.5 miles along an old woods road to a junction with the blue trail. Stay left. The forest is thick with hemlock in the shadows of Indian Head Mountain, which rises to 3,573 feet above. A good snowpack is usually found on this northern slope by mid-winter. Follow the red markers as the road dissipates to a footpath at 0.7 miles; there may be several short difficult spots where you must take off your skis. When the trail joins the Old Overlook Road at 1.95 miles, you have crossed the most difficult sections. Make a right uphill along the old road, and pass the Devil's Path on right. Follow blue markers to the lean-to at 2.1 miles. This open area next to a bubbling creek is a good spot to break and evaluate your progress.

Climbing skins attached to the bottom of telemark skis help on a climb.

From the lean-to, the trail crosses a bridge and rises moderately following the blue markers. Several washouts mar the road here so circumnavigate the best you can. At 2.6 miles the trail swings to a southerly direction and views across the Hudson Valley to the east open up. A yellow trail to the left meanders easily a short distance to a viewpoint by an old quarry. (This new trail may not show up on maps.) The town below and to the east along the Hudson is Saugerties.

The blue trail continues along the escarpment over a level road at 2,500 feet. The trail base is very smooth, so even with little snow in this sunny exposure skiing is possible. At 3.5 miles, Skunk Spring is on the right. If it is past noon in mid-winter you may want to end the trip here because of the long journey ahead.

At 4.5 miles the trail passes the yellow Echo Lake Trail, which descends to the right 0.6 miles to the lake. The Old Overlook Road continues over easy grades and then begins to rise to the junction with red Overlook Trail after a long 5.9 miles. Making a left will bring you 0.5 miles to the fire tower to the east. Going right a short distance from the junction will bring you to the hotel ruins. (The road continues down from here 2.0 miles to the Meads parking area across from a monastery.)

When returning on the Old Overlook Road, it is very important to catch the arrow and the red trail to Predigar Road 0.2 miles after the lean-to on the left. There are several logs across the road, but they may be covered in deep snow, so beware. Going straight past this junction brings you through the Platte Clove Preserve, 1.0 miles to Platte Clove Road; however, winter hiking is not permitted due to dangerous conditions. Come back in the summer to check out the waterfalls and a little red house where the novelist and adventurer Jack London is said to have stayed.

2. MINK HOLLOW

Intermediate-Expert

Cross-Country
Telemark
Snowshoe

If you want a sunny outing up a deep mountain hollow not too far from civilization, the Mink Hollow Trail may be it. It follows an old wagon road dating back to the 1790s. The route was for carrying hides from as far away as South America to the leather-tanning factories of Tannersville and Edwardsville (now Hunter). The bark of the hemlock tree was needed for this process; the result was decimation of the hemlock, which once accounted for over 25 percent of the forest north of the Mink Hollow notch. Today there is much restoration of the tree in the Catskills, although ancient stands are hard to find.

This trail is perhaps best approached from the south, or Lake Hill area, as there is room for several cars at the turnaround at the end of Mink Hollow Road. The first mile or so of the trail is easy and bringing along a novice skier to this point is appropriate. This north-south trail offers abundant sunshine on frigid but clear days. Approaching the trail from the north at Elka Park can be a bit daunting. It is a shorter but steeper climb to the lean-to. The distance between trailheads is 4.3 miles. To park cars at both ends requires driving 45 minutes through Phoenicia up to Tannersville.

Getting There

For Lake Hill: Leave the village green in Woodstock and go west 2.0 miles on NY Route 212 to Bearsville. Stay right over bridge. At 5.0 miles make a right after the Lake Hill post office onto Mink Hollow Road. Proceed north 2.85 miles to the end-of-the-road turnaround, where there is room for several cars.

For Elka Park: From the traffic light and NY Route 23A in Tannersville, travel south on County Route 16.

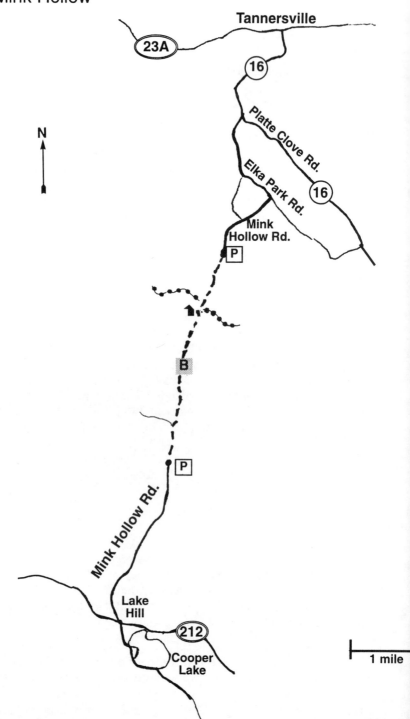

At 1.3 miles, bear left at Bloomer road. At 1.8 miles make a right onto Elka Road. Go another 1.4 miles and make a right onto Mink Hollow Road. Proceed another 1.4 miles toward the trailhead. Park your vehicle at least 0.1 miles before the trailhead.

The Trail The trail from the Lake Hill approach follows blue DEC trail markers from the turnaround. As the road is cobbled in many spots, with numerous springs and bubbling brooks to cross, a good frozen base with a deeper snowpack makes skiing this route more enjoyable. After steep grades, the height of the land is reached at 2.8 miles at an elevation of 2,600 feet. At 2.95 miles there is a lean-to on the left that might offer welcome shelter in this windy col (a space or pass through a low spot in a ridge or between two mountains). At 3.05 miles, the trail crosses Devil's Path, which leads left to Plateau Mountain and right to Sugarloaf Mountain, both rising to over 3,800 feet. These trails are strictly for rock and ice climbers. The old wagon road travels down gradual grades 0.8 miles over a northern exposure to the Elka Park trailhead.

3 • Kaaterskill High Peak

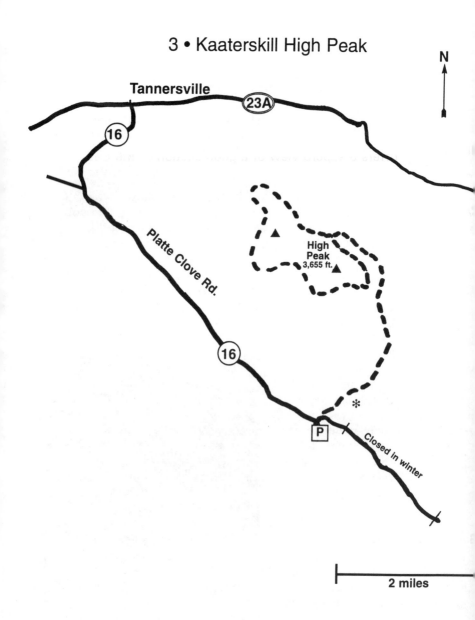

3. KAATERSKILL HIGH PEAK

Intermediate-Expert

**Cross-Country
Telemark
Snowshoe**

The drive west across the Kingston-Rhinecliff Bridge offers a superb view of a good section of the Catskills. Ahead is the escarpment with its sharp rise out of the Hudson Valley. The one mountain that stands out is Kaaterskill High Peak (sometimes listed as High Peak) with its dramatic 3,655-foot summit. Long ago, it was thought to be the tallest peak in the Catskills; more accurate surveying methods in the 1800s determined that 21 other mountains in the Catskills are higher.

Today, a snowmobile trail from the top of Platte Clove reaches to within 500 feet of the summit of Kaaterskill High Peak and wraps around its sister peak, Roundtop Mountain. For much of the journey, the old woods road is through a southern exposure, which might be warming for a mid-winter jaunt on a sunny day. A good snow base of a foot or more is recommended, as the first part of the trail has a cobbled base. Because of snowmobile traffic and limited parking, weekdays may be a better time to ski this trail. Platte Clove Road, which descends along a canyon to West Saugerties, is also used by skiers and snowmobilers.

Getting There

The trailhead is located on County Route 16, 0.9 miles east of Predigar Road. (See "Getting There," page page 30.) Note that Platte Clove Road from West Saugerties is closed from November 15 to April 15. The parking area and turn-around are where the road closes for the winter.

The Trail

The trail begins at about 1,800 feet and rises moderately, following orange snowmobile-trail markers. This is a good section for trying out climbing skins as there is a moderate climb on a trail usually packed down by snowmobiles. There are several woods roads after 1.0 mile that lead to private property so bear right following the trail markers. (A short distance, at 1.1 miles on a bend, a trail veers off to Huckleberry Point, 1.3 miles away. There are several difficult sections along this trail so telemark skis or showshoes are suggested to travel to a precipice that offers spectacular views of Platte Clove and the Hudson Valley. Be sure to follow the trail markers closely as precipices are very dangerous.) The main trail continues north through varying grades of difficulty until, at 2.3 miles, the land levels at 3,000 feet in elevation. There are dramatic views of Overlook, Plattekill, Indian Head, and Twin Mountains to the south.

The trail continues over more level ground through thick balsam and fir to a junction at 3.5 miles where the snowmobile trail makes a sharp left. At 3.7 miles, a DEC sign indicates the beginning of a 7.6-miles loop around Rountop and High Peak. This is a good spot to evaluate your progress and stamina. The loop weaves in and out of the 3,000-foot level over a long course. To ski the complete loop back to Platte Clove loop should qualify you for the next Winter Olympics!

Kaaterskill High Peak from the Hudson Valley.

4. NORTH LAKE

All Levels

No Fee in Winter

Cross-Country Telemark Snowshoe

Perhaps no other section of the Catskill Forest Preserve is so rich in history as is the North Lake region. Once two separate lakes, North Lake and South Lake are now connected by a narrow channel. They are nestled between North and South Mountains along the escarpment in the northeastern Catskills. Native Americans referred to the escarpment as the Great Wall of Manitou, after the spirit, Manitou, who they believed existed there. This area was the hunting ground for the tribes that lived below in the Hudson Valley. As European settlers began to arrive in the seventeenth century, the forbidding nature of the lake area began to draw a few of the more curious settlers.

In 1741, John Bartram, a well-known botanist from Philadelphia, set out on one of several trips to the North Lake area to collect balsam fir specimens, also known as the balm of Gilead, the tree believed to be the one that the ancient Israelites found on Mount Gilead in the Holy Land. The spruce trees found growing with the balsam fir led to another endeavor in the 1790s, when entrepreneur John Ashley fermented their tips to make spruce beer. About the same time, landscape painter Thomas Cole, who went on to found the Hudson River School, painted many Catskill scenes, including the popular Kaaterskill Falls below the outlet of South Lake. The fifth-highest Catskill peak, just north in the Blackhead Range, is named after him. William Cullen Bryant, Henry David Thoreau, Jack London, and others spent time in this region, about the same time adding their voices to the birth of American literary Romanticism.

The hotel era began in the 1820s with the arrival of the Catskill Mountain House. Situated just above what is now the North Lake beach area, it grew to become a large building with a Greek Revival facade.

4 • North Lake

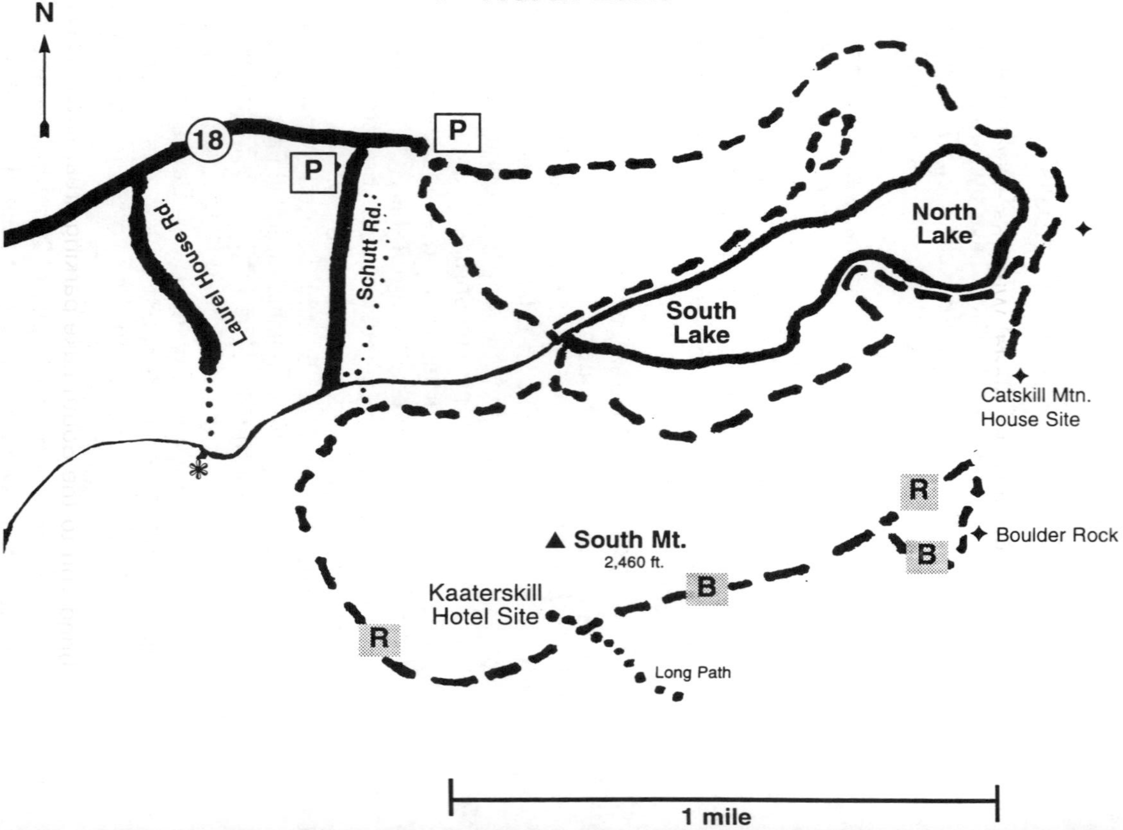

N

18

Laurel House Rd.

Schutt Rd.

P

P

North Lake

South Lake

Catskill Mtn. House Site

▲ South Mt. 2,460 ft.

Kaaterskill Hotel Site

Long Path

Boulder Rock

R

B

B

R

*

1 mile

Commanding views of the valley 2,000 feet below made it a popular resort by the 1870s, and many of the elite of the time, including four presidents, visited there. On the top of South Mountain, the Hotel Kaaterskill emerged; brochures boasted it was the largest mountain hotel in the world. With the arrival of the railroad in the late 1800s, many more hotels and large rooming houses were established. Today most are closed and their remains have fallen into disrepair.

The North Lake campground was first developed in 1929. It has expanded over the years to include South Lake. A dam on the outlet of South Lake raised the water enough to create one large lake. A variable complex of auto roads, old carriage roads and hiking trails makes the area an excellent choice for cross-country skiing and snowshoeing. The summer months bring throngs of campers and day visitors; however, skiers may have trails all to themselves. Next to North Lake, at an elevation of 2,150 feet, are views to the east of five states on an exceptionally clear day. A winter trek to the Hotel Kaaterskill site opens a sweeping panorama to the south and west from a wide mountaintop meadow. Snowmobiles are permitted only in certain designated areas of the park.

Getting There From south and east: Most common use is Exit 20 of the New York State Thruway (I-87) at Saugerties. Follow Route 32 north for approximately 6 miles to Route 32A to Route 23A west. Proceed up 23A to Haines Falls. Make the first right turn in the village of Haines Falls onto County Route 18 and travel 2 miles to the end of the road, where there is a registration booth (closed in winter). The first right after the booth will bring you to the South Lake parking area. After heavy snowfalls, this may not be plowed immediately; in that case, park by the registration booth. There is a general store with ski rentals at the beginning of the county road on left. There are several ski and hiking shops in nearby Tannersville. No restroom or facilities are available at North Lake in the winter months.

The Trails

The approach to the trails depends on whether you park by the registration booth (gatehouse) or at the South lake parking area. After heavy snowfalls people park by the booth. Skiing by the barrier gate straight ahead brings you along the north perimeter of the two lakes. There are many loops to explore. After 1.5 miles swing south along the east side of North Lake. There are views along the escarpment to the left, near the beach buildings. Some wind intensity is common when approaching this area so dress appropriately. From the beach parking area, ski to the south and look for blue trail markers which guide you to the Catskill Mountain House site, 0.2 miles up a short hill, where there are more fine views of several states to the east. Returning to the road allows you to complete the loop around the south side of the lakes.

Skiing from the South Lake parking area has several ability options. There is a nice, easy trail leading along the north shore to the ranger house, by the inlet to North Lake. Going south from the dam along the road brings you to a winter hiking trail 0.1 miles in on your right. Look for the nordic ski trail markers. This novice trail follows an old carriage road for 0.4 miles west to the junction of several trails. Making a left on the red Schutt Road Trail will bring you to the site of the Hotel Kaaterskill. The trail rises moderately for 0.2 miles and if the novice can manage this, the rest will be easy. The trail curves around to the south side of the mountain, over easy grades to the next junction at 1.1 miles. A left just before the junction on a un-marked trail up the hill will bring you to the hotel site, where skiing in the large meadows at 2,450 feet gives good views of High Peak and Roundtop Mountains to the south. This is a good spot to snack or break for lunch in the sun.

Returning to the trail, ski to the left along the blue Escarpment Trail for 0.6 miles to the next junction to the east. Keep right along the blue trail for 0.2 miles for Boulder Rock Lookout, where there are marvelous views south to the Hudson Valley below. In the distance are the Shawangunk Mountains above New Paltz. The trail returns the same way.

The Kaaterskill Falls at any time of the year is a true natural wonder. The highest falls in New York State, it actually consists of two tiers: the upper falls drop 175 feet and the lower one 85 feet. Leaving the registration booth by car, look for Laurel House Road on left after 0.5 miles. Make a left and go 0.5 miles to the parking area (if plowed). Ski or snowshoe from the yellow barrier gate south along the path 0.2 miles to the top of the falls. Standing at the edge of the precipice is dangerous any time of the year, and especially so in the winter. Many fatalities have occurred here. Don't become part of Catskill history!

Birch grove at Hotel Kaaters-·kill site.

5. MOUNTAIN TRAILS TOURING CENTER

All Levels

Full Service

Trail Fee

Recommended for Children

Located off NY Route 23A near Tannersville, this 300-acre nordic ski center, at a base elevation of 1,800 feet, has one of the largest trail systems in the Northeast. Most of the 35 kilometers of trails were old logging roads that have been upgraded to make fine bases for cross-country skiing. They are groomed, track set and marked according to ability. The trails are well patrolled and a full sales and rental shop is located on the premises.

Tannersville, named for the tanneries that once flourished here, has many hotels and bed and breakfasts for an overnight stay. Hunter Mountain is located several miles farther west, so there are plenty of restaurants and other night life activities in the area.

Getting There

From Exit 20 on the Thruway at Saugerties: Proceed north on Route 32 to Route 32A to Route 23A west to the traffic light in Tannersville. Travel 0.5 miles and look for sign on right for Mountain Trails.

From the north: From Exit 21 of the Thruway at Catskill: Go east on Route 23 to 9W south to 23A west to Tannersville.

More info.

Call (518) 589-5361 or write Mountain Trails, Box 198, Route 23A, Tannersville, NY 12485

6. COLGATE LAKE

**Beginner-
Intermediate**

*Cross-Country
Telemark
Snowshoe*

This under-used trail offers an excellent cross section of Catskill forests. It is an ideal location for a beginner skier, as the first part of the trail is in a huge, relatively flat meadow. This land was once owned by Robert Colgate of the Colgate Palmolive Company, but much of it is now state-owned Catskill Forest Preserve. In the nineteenth century, a wagon road to Dutcher Notch and over to the village of Catskill was the prime way to get goods in and out of this 2,000-foot valley.

Hovering above the entrance meadow are the peaks of highly visible Black Head Range—containing the third-, fourth-, and fifth-highest peaks in the Catskills—all just shy of 4,000 feet. The trail to the pond above Lake Capra is a good 2.2 miles each way. The trail to Dutcher Notch is a full-day trip, which requires careful planning and which should be attempted only by the expert leaving in the early morning. There is a small general store and post office in the town of East Jewett.

**A pond along
the Colgate
Lake Trail.**

6 • Colgate Lake

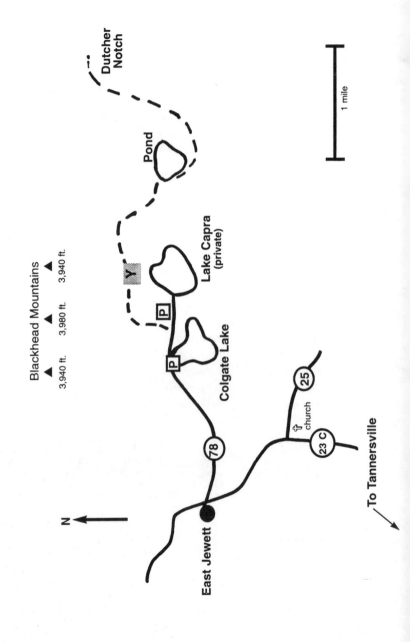

Dutcher Notch

Pond

Blackhead Mountains

▲ 3,940 ft.   ▲ 3,980 ft.   ▲ 3,940 ft.

Y

P

P

Lake Capra
(private)

Colgate Lake

N

78

25

church

23 C

East Jewett

To Tannersville

1 mile

Getting There
From the Tannersville light and Route 23A, travel north up hill on County Route 23C for 4.8 miles and make a right on to County Route 78, across from the East Jewett post office. Proceed 1.7 miles east past Colgate Lake, with the waterfall on right, to the third DEC parking area on the left. (There is a large parking area, but maintenance of this lot is unpredictable in heavier snowfalls, so be prepared to park on the little-used road.)

The Trail
From the barrier gate in the parking area, follow the yellow trail markers along a hedge north toward Black Dome Mountain. It is important to constantly watch for the trail markers—there are many old roads and trails weaving in an out of this system. At 0.2 miles the trail enters a deciduous forest where you sign in at the trail register. After relatively flat terrain, the trail turns abruptly left at 0.9 miles and the base becomes rockier for a while—a good spot for the novice to turn around. At the small ravine at 1.2 miles remove your skis to cross the small stream feeding into Lake Capra. The trail resumes on an old woodland road. The large pond at 2.2 miles is a good spot to break for lunch and take some photos. The forest here becomes thick with balsam, hemlock and pine, and is more akin to a northern Maine forest. It is best to stay off the ice on the lake because there are numerous springs along the shore. For the less-hardy skier, this is a good spot to turn back. Where the trail joins the old road from Lake Capra go left toward Dutcher Notch. At 4.2 miles it joins the Escarpment Trail, where some fine vistas can be seen.

7. DIAMOND NOTCH

Intermediate-Expert

Cross-Country
Telemark
Snowshoe

The Diamond Notch trail begins at the end of a long, bucolic valley winding past old farms and Grange halls and follows an old wagon road through a high, narrow notch between two of the Catskills' larger mountains. It must have been a difficult road for wagons to cross, because it is snowed in at the notch most years from November through April. The road is percipitous in spots, especially on the southern Lanesville approach. It is best skied from the Spruceton or northern trail-head, where there are more options for different levels of skiers. Upon reaching the notch, there are impressive views to the south toward the Burroughs Range (Slide, Cornell, Wittenberg) and viewing them in winter is the best time from this location. The old road is very cobbled, and may be deeply rutted in spots, so a good snowpack is recommended to ski this trail. Spring is an especially pleasant time to ski here; a good snowpack is usually found on the northern side.

Getting There

From NY Routes 28 and 42 in Shandaken: Travel 7.4 miles north on Route 42 to hamlet of Westkill on right. Turn right on Spruceton Road (County Road 6) and proceed 6.7 miles to large DEC parking area on left. (At 6.9 miles there is another DEC parking area on the right, which is closer to trailhead.) Park at whichever lot is plowed. At 7.0 miles at barrier gate and turn-around there is no parking from November to April.

The Trail

The trail begins at the barrier gate at an elevation of 2,000 feet in the shadows of Westkill Mountain, sixth-highest in the Catskills. The old road follows a stream to your right over easy grades. In a clearing at 0.7 miles several trails meet. Novice skiers should end their trip here, but not before peeking at lovely Dia-

7 • Diamond Notch

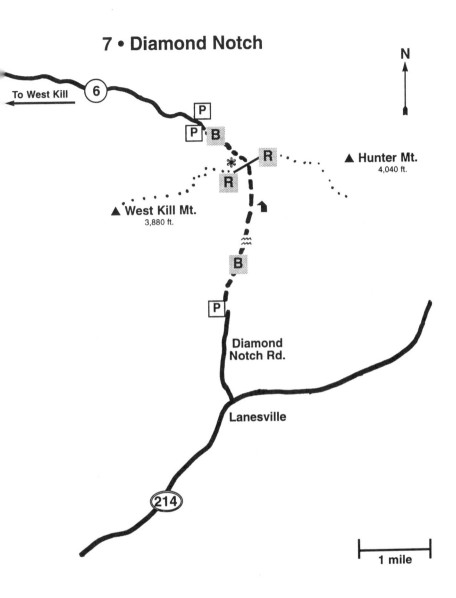

N

To West Kill

6

P

P B

* R

R

▲ Hunter Mt.
4,040 ft.

▲ West Kill Mt.
3,880 ft.

B

P

Diamond
Notch Rd.

Lanesville

214

1 mile

mond Notch Falls to the right, by the footbridge. You will notice the bulletin board and sign-in at the register. The good intermediate or expert skier can proceed from this four-way junction by crossing the bridge over the falls and making a left, following the blue markers. The trail rises over moderate, winding grades to the lean-to at 1.4 miles. A short jaunt to the height of the land brings you to an elevation of 2,650 feet. Powerful winds funneling through here stunt and warp the tree growth. A deep snowpack of 6 feet or more is common by early April. Caution must be used here in very cold, windy weather due to exposure of ice.

At 1.5 miles views to the south open up. For those wanting to continue, the road drops rather steeply for a while, and top expert skills are required. The road is completely washed out at the next bridge. At 3.4 miles is the barrier gate of the Lanesville side. Parking your car at the Lanesville end is less dependable, because plowing is unpredictable. Do not park your vehicle by last the house on the road. Driving time between trailheads is 45 minutes.

8. UTSAYANTHA TRAIL SYSTEM

All Levels

Cross-Country
Telemark
Snowshoe

Driving east to west on NY Route 23 in the northern Catskills near Windham brings you across the deepest gorges and alongside some of the highest peaks. At Grand Gorge, the terrain changes to a more gentle topography, with farm silos rather than high peaks on the horizon. A patchwork of fields and forest signals the end of the northwest Catskills at Stamford. This area is indicative of what most of the Catskills were like 100 years ago when farming was the main occupation and many of the smaller mountains were cleared to their summits for pasture. Most of the eastern Catskills have returned to forest now, and the only remnants of past farm life are the many stone walls often hidden by vegetation.

The historic town of Stamford, settled in the late 1700s, has a unique character of its own and is dubbed "Queen of the Catskills." Dominating the landscape is Mount Utsayantha, named after an Indian princess. According to legend, she loved a white settler and bore a child by him. Utsayantha's angry father drowned the baby, and the grief-stricken mother committed suicide by jumping into Lake Utsayantha from atop the mountain. In the late 1800s, promoters used this story to attract tourists to the growing hotel industry in the area. An observation building, looking much like a lighthouse, was erected on the summit of Mount Utsayantha; it still stands next to the state fire tower and cabin. Viewing the landscape from this vantage point, one can see the agricultural mosaic in the valleys below, especially to the west. To the south and east, spectacular views of almost all the Catskill high peaks can be seen from several clearings on or near the summit. On a crisp, clear day, the Green Mountains of Vermont are in the distance, as well as the

8 • Utsayantha Trails

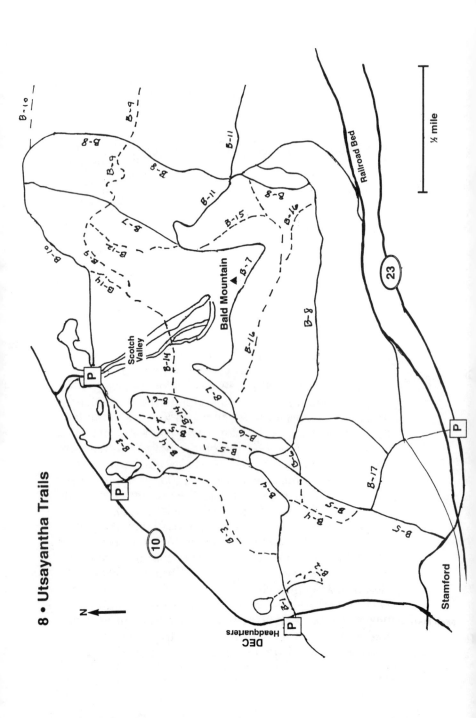

Adirondack Mountains to the north. An area of 20,000 sqaure miles is said to be visible from here!

The Utsayantha Trail System lies in the valleys below, and offers excellent cross-country skiing. Winding through private lands through the cooperation of the townships of Stamford, Jefferson and Harpersfield, the trails have been designed to provide enjoyment to all outdoor enthusiasts, which is rare for the Catskill region. There are a total of more than 50 miles to cross-country ski, from grassy old woods roads to a reconditioned 20-mile railbed trail. Because the trails are laid out on private lands, their status may change. Scotch Valley ski area is a good place to enter into the system; information and rentals are available there. Another good place to park is the trailhead across from the regional DEC headquarters just north of Stamford.

Getting There

Stamford is located approximately a half hour east of Oneonta on NY Route 23 or an hour west of Catskill on NY Route 23. A popular spot to enter the trail system is by the barrier gate next to Russ Archibald Park, directly across from the Regional DEC headquarters on Route 10, 1 mile north of the intersection of Routes 23 and 10. Scotch Valley ski resort is 1.4 miles farther up Route 10 on the right.

The Trails

The network of trails is too vast to describe easily. There are red markers (with letters and numbers) on most of the trails; however, some of the markers are in disrepair or missing. Most of the trails lie between Route 23 and Route 10, so you are never too far from an access road. This is one area where a compass

Map Note: The solid lines are multi-use trails.

may come in handy: If you are in doubt as to your location, it can help you back to the trailhead. The railbed following Routes 23 and 10 and swinging southwest from Stamford is a good trail for beginners when there is sufficient snow. There are many access points in and around the village of Stamford. Trails going southwest along the lakes from Scotch Valley are reasonably easy as they move through mixed hardwoods to evergreens with many sunny meadows.

A Note about Mount Utsayantha A snowshoe or winter hike up to the 3,365 summit of Mount Utsayantha is well worth the climb—the views are among the best, if not *the* best, in the Catskills. However, the trail follows a dirt road up a steady incline and requires expert skills.

To reach Mount Utsayantha, start from the light at the intersection of Routes 10 and 23, proceed east on Route 23 for 0.8 miles and make right on Mountain Avenue. Travel up the hill, which becomes steep for 1.2 miles, until the road levels. Look for a road to the left and park off to the side. After passing a private drive to the right, the road soon climbs, winding 1 mile to the summit. Respect all posted lands along the length of the trail. At the summit there is a large clearing; it makes a fine spot to break for lunch and look through a pair of binoculars. Oh yes: Bring a camera.

Old observation tower on the summit of Mount Utsayantha

9. MINE KILL STATE PARK

All Levels

Recommend for Children

ross-country
Snowshoe
Tobogganing
Sledding
'isitor Center

This state park and adjacent Blenheim-Gilboa Power Project Visitor Center overlooking a large reservoir has many activities to offer besides cross-country skiing. There are many hands-on displays in the red barn operated by the New York Power Authority. This is an ideal place to bring children. Eagles may be spotted flying above the reservoir and can be viewed through telescopes from inside. There is a vast terrain for winter activities.

etting There

From the south at Grand Gorge at the intersection of NY Routes 23 and 30: proceed 7 miles north on Route 30 and watch for signs to the Visitor Center. From Albany: take Interstate 90 west to Interstate 88. Go south on 88 to the exit for NY Route 30 and Scoharie. Proceed south on 30 for 28 miles.

More info.

For more information, call 1-800-724-0309.

Blenheim-Gilboa ower Project isitor Center

10. BALSAM LAKE MOUNTAIN

Intermediate-Expert

Cross-country
Telemark
Snowshoe

This tall mountain, named for the small lake it hovers over to the south, has an old jeep road climbing the north slopes for 3 miles, eventually curving up to an restored fire tower at 3,723 feet. Spectacular views reward any skier or snowshoer who can climb a landing or two on the fire tower. What makes this trail unique is after an initial short, steep climb, much of the trail has gentle grades above 3,000 feet in elevation, therefore, a decent snowpack is assured for much of the winter. This makes for fine spring skiing, too.

Getting There

From NY Route 28 in Arkville: Turn onto Dry Brook Road (County Route 49) and travel 6.1 miles; there is a wooden road-maintenance shed on right. Make a right on Millbrook Road and proceed 2.3 miles up moderate grade to the top of the road and look for a DEC parking area on the right. There is room for several cars; however, if it's not plowed, park well off the road.

The Trail

At the DEC parking area there is a bulletin board with a trail map and other interesting information. This is one of the highest base elevations of all the trails. It begins across the road and pitches up for a short distance to the register box. From here the road follows blue trail markers over easy-to-moderate grades. At 2.2 miles from the start is the intersection with the red trail to the right. For the more adventurous, the blue trail continues over the ridge and then descends into the Upper Beaverkill Valley for two miles to a DEC parking area. The red trail climbs 0.75 miles to the summit and fire tower of Balsam Lake Mountain. Ex-

10 • Balsam Lake Mountain

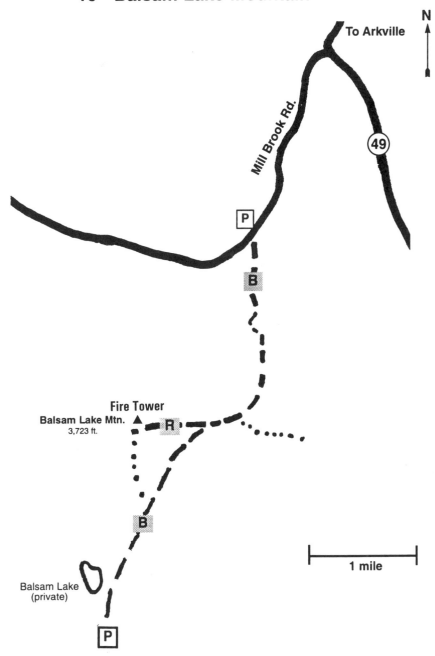

pect heavy snow and slow climbing on this north face of the summit, which is thick with balsam trees. At the summit looking east is Graham and Doubletop Mountains with Slide between them. You have come 3 miles from Millbrook Road, and it is a challenging glide back to the parking area. The less-skilled skier may want to walk or sideslip the initial descent.

11. BELLEAYRE MOUNTAIN

All Levels

Recommended for Children

Cross-country
Telemark
Snowshoe
Downhill

This state-run facility, part alpine and part nordic, is a very popular and convenient destination. Located at 2,000 feet, the area is blessed with abundant snow. In one of the prime snowbelt areas of the Catskills, the cross-country area offers more than 9.0 kilometers of trails for all abilities and is open to the public at no charge.

The nordic trail system is located within sight of the Discovery (lower) Lodge at the downhill area. The Overlook (upper) Lodge boasts one of the highest base elevations of any ski area in the East at 2,541 feet. It is also one of the oldest ski areas in the East. The upper lodge was built in 1949 in classic log-cabin style and has been modified several times over the years. From this lodge, there is an impressive view of the mountains to the north, including Bearpen and West-kill.

Much of the area was developed during the railroad era of the late nineteenth century and in its heyday there were many large hotels in the vicinity, most of which have since burned or vanished. However, in the nearby hamlet of Pine Hill, several smaller inns still exist, including the Pine Hill Arms and the Colonial Inn, which continue to offer lodging. A mile to the west, in Fleischmanns, several large rooming houses have survived as quaint bed and breakfasts, and motel accommodations are plentiful. Located within walking distance to the cross-country trails is the Belleayre Ski Shop. It has been in continuous operation for 40 years, having been transferred from the upper mountain in the late 1970s. It carries a full range of rental equipment, waxes and other nordic accessories.

Because of their popularity and convenient location, the Belleayre trails are usually well tracked within days of a snowfall, but on weekdays you may be the only one out there. There is no grooming or ski patrol. The H trail skirts the Discovery Lodge, where all services and amenities are found.

Getting There From exit 19 of the Thruway in Kingston, travel 40 miles west on NY Route 28 to Highmount, at the top of the long hill. Make a left to the Belleayre Mountain Ski Area and proceed 0.2 miles, past the post office and Belleayre Ski Shop, to the large sign on the left indicating the cross-country area. Turn left and you will find a large, well-maintained parking area 100 yards on the right.

The Trails There is a large trail sign visible from the parking lot. The A trails and the large open field next to the parking area are good for novices. The H and J trails have steeper turns too advanced for beginners. As the Catskill Forest Preserve is dominated here by many maple trees, with a sprinkling of beech and hemlock, it is generally a sunny outing on a clear day. There is no charge for the use of the trails.

More info. Maps may be obtained at the lodges or at the Belleayre Ski Shop down the hill. Call (845)254-5600 for snow conditions; (845)254-5338 for the Belleayre Ski Shop.

12 • Rochester Hollow

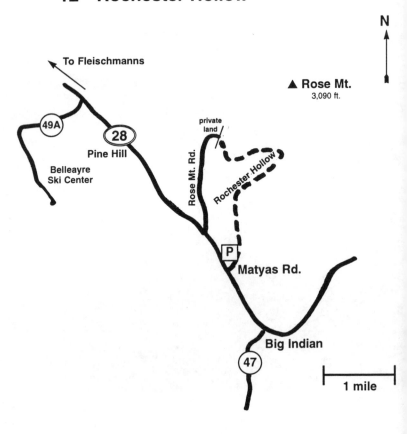

N

To Fleischmanns

▲ **Rose Mt.**
3,090 ft.

49A

28

Pine Hill

Belleayre
Ski Center

private
land

Rose Mt. Rd.

Rochester Hollow

P

Matyas Rd.

Big Indian

47

1 mile

12. ROCHESTER HOLLOW

Intermediate

**Cross-country
Telemark
Snowshoe**

An old woods road to Rochester Hollow offers an excellent and little-used alternative to the facilities at nearby Belleayre Mountain. It makes a good mid-winter climb; there is plenty of sunshine through a mostly deciduous forest, with a southern exposure for 3 miles to the end of state land. It is right off NY Route 28, and there are several general stores nearby where you can obtain provisions for an afternoon outing. Close by is the quaint hamlet of Pine Hill; over the hill past Belleayre Mountain is the village of Fleischmanns in Delaware County.

Getting There

From the intersection of NY Route 28 and County Route 47 in Big Indian (by the general store), proceed west on Route 28 for 1.1 miles toward Pine Hill. Make a right on Matyas Road and proceed 0.1 miles to stone the columns, where there is parking for several cars. If the road is plowed past the columns, travel 0.1 miles farther to a barrier gate, where there is additional parking.

The Trail

Beginning at about the 1,300-foot level and following a bubbling brook to the left, the trail base is generally easy on the ski bottoms, and skiing possible on as little as six inches of snow. Approximately 2 miles after winding and rising gradually, you'll reach another set of stone columns and the trail rises moderately. It soon turns sharply to the west and follows more level terrain to the end of the trail and state land at 3.0 miles. (The old road continues on over private land for 0.2 miles where it joins Rose Mountain Road.)

13 • Alder Lake

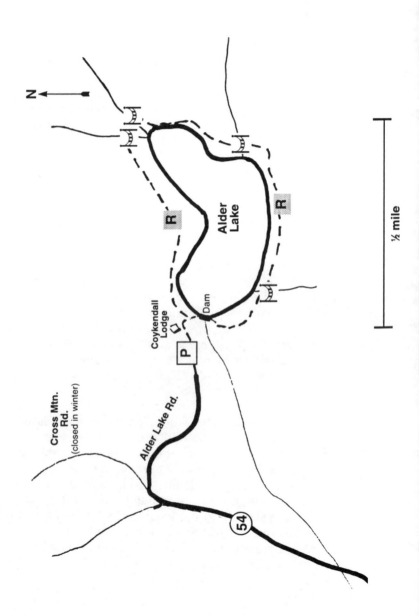

N

Cross Mtn.
Rd.
(closed in winter)

Alder Lake Rd.

Coykendall
Lodge

P

Dam

R

Alder
Lake

R

54

½ mile

13. ALDER LAKE

Intermediate

Cross-country
Snowshoe

The Alder Lake loop is an easy 1.5-mile trail around one of the higher lakes in the Catskills. Located at 2,200 feet, it is one of many lakes in this section created by a small dam and exclusively used in the past by hunting and fishing clubs. As you approach the lake you can't help but notice Coykendall Lodge, built by George Coykendall, general superintendent of the Ulster & Delaware Railroad. The building, which once boasted all the conveniences of a first-class hotel, is now part of the Catskill Forest Preserve. It is also one of the more isolated places to ski, so proper preparation is necessary.

Getting There

From NY Route 28 and the Margaretville Bridge: Drive west on Route 28 for 2.3 miles. Make a left at the sign for Reservoir Road, then make an immediate right. Proceed 8.6 miles farther along New York City Road to Barkaboom Road. Go left. Drive 6.4 miles up and over the mountain ridge and make a left on Beaverkill Road at intersection. Proceed 1.5 miles and make a left just over a bridge onto Alder Lake Road (County Route 54). Continue for 2.3 miles up the road and bear right at a fork watching for signs. There is a barrier gate, and this where you will have to park unless it is open and plowed.

From NY Route 17 (Quickway): Take Exit 96 at Livingston Manor and turn onto Sullivan County Route 179 north toward Deckertown and Lewbeach. In 1.2 miles turn right onto Sullivan County Route 151 (Johnson Hill Road) toward Beaverkill. Drive for 4.1 miles (Sullivan County 151 turns into Sullivan County 152); continue straight for 4 miles, where the road becomes Ulster County Route 54. Continue on for 3 to Turnwood. Follow directions above from Turnwood.

The Trail   Ski or hike up a road for 0.3 miles to the summer parking area and trail register. This is the most challenging climb for the whole course. Follow the trail a short distance past the Coykendall Lodge on the left and proceed down grade to the shore area and dam to the right. From this location, the 1.5-mile loop begins either way. The trail follows red trail markers and the general contour of the lake. There are several small bridges to cross over the feeder streams as well as some woods roads that branch off from the trail and might be fun to explore. Northwest and looming over the lake is the Millbrook Ridge which rises to more than 3,000 feet.

14. KELLY HOLLOW

Intermediate-Expert

**Cross-country
Telemark
Snowshoe**

This newly designated nordic ski trail takes you on an excursion to a mountain pond high along a ridge. Bordering on two counties, the trailhead is along one of the most bucolic roads in the area. Many remnants of past farm life can be pondered when skiing along this trail that begins at a 1,700-foot base. Above the valley is the Millbrook Ridge, 4 miles long, all of it over 3,000 feet. The trail, itself an old road, winds along several stream courses, and if the intermediate skier can get past the initial steep grades, it should not be a problem reaching the height of the land, where there is a beaver pond and a nearby lean-to. Although there is no view from the higher elevation, the rewards are the unusual topography and highly diverse forest. The trail base is eroded in sections so a substantial snow cover of a foot or more is ideal. This area is isolated and the few houses along Millbrook Road may be just summer retreats, so prepare well. Because of its isolation and infrequent use, skiing it alone is not recommended.

Getting There

From NY Route 28 and the Magaretville Bridge: Travel west 2.3 miles on Route 28. Make left past sign for Reservoir road, then make immediate right. Go 3.9 miles on NYC Reservoir Road to Millbrook Road on left. Make left and proceed 5.5 miles; look for signs for parking area on right; there is room for 10 cars. An outhouse is next to the parking area.

The Trails

From the rear of the parking area, sign in at the trail register and follow the yellow nordic trail markers to the barrier gate.

14• Kelly Hollow

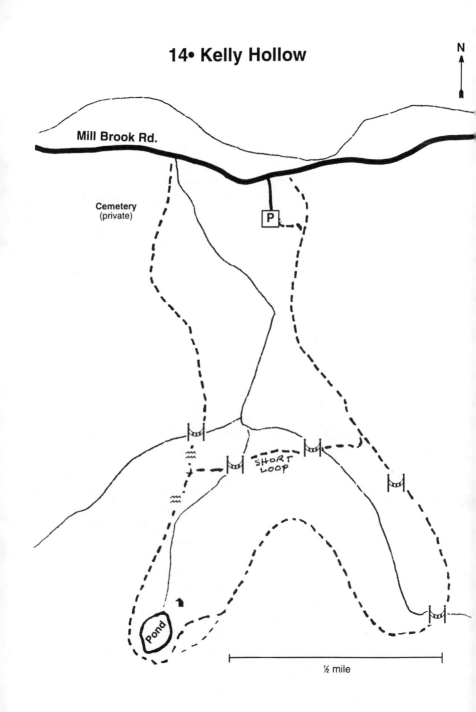

N

Mill Brook Rd.

Cemetery
(private)

P

SHORT
LOOP

Pond

½ mile

The old woods road rises gently amid old stone walls. After 0.3 miles, the trail grades becomes steeper on a rutted sub-surface to the short loop junction at 0.6 miles. Here the intermediate skier should not be discouraged—continue straight ahead on the long loop, as the steepest grades have already been passed. (Making a right for the short loop will bring you down into a ravine with many difficult but interesting sections. The short loop rejoins the long loop at the 2.6-mile point). Continuing up the long loop brings you up easy grades through bogs and to a thick, mature Norway spruce forest that is spellbinding. On a warm spring day, it is still an icebox in this brief section of the trail.

At 1.0 miles, the trail crosses a bridge at a hairpin turn and rises slowly to the west, then veers back north on more moderate grades, finally reaching the lean-to at 1.9 miles. Approach the pond quietly and you may catch a glimpse of some of the wildlife that are attracted to this large opening in the hollow. The pond is 450 feet above the trailhead, but even in winter it is hard to find a view because the Millbrook Ridge wraps around this area.

From here, the intermediate skier may want to go back the same way, as the rest of the long loop has steeper grades over a shorter distance. The expert can follow the trail markers around the pond, then descend past some old settlements to the left before the junction with the short loop at 2.6 miles. It continues on with steeper grades in spots before leveling out after 3 miles. At the barrier gate at 3.3 miles there is an old but still-used cemetery to the left. Skiing a short distance farther will bring you back to Millbrook Road; the parking area is 0.3 miles along the road to the right (east).

15 • Mongaup-Willowemoc

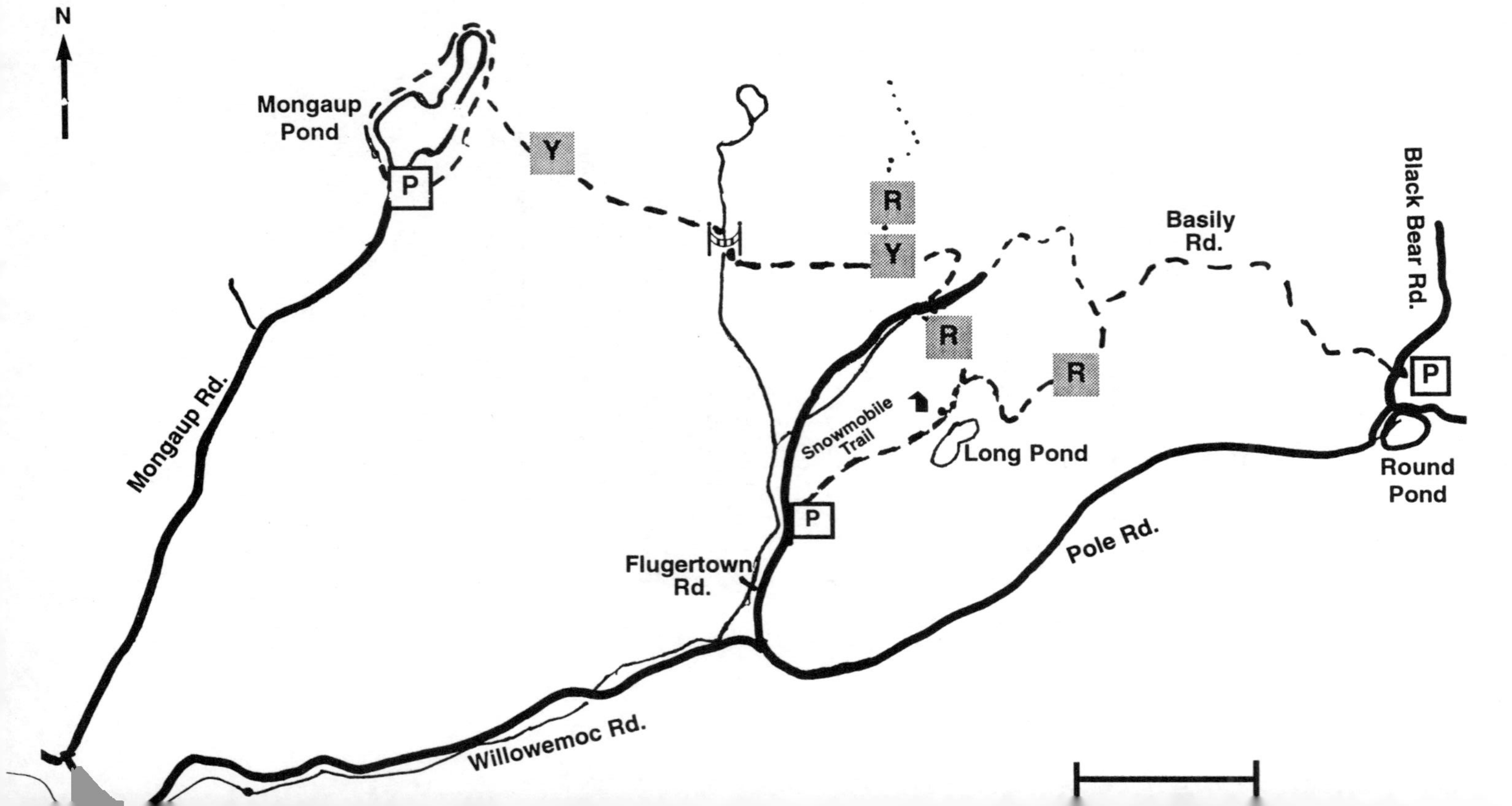

Black Bear Rd.

P

Round Pond

Basily Rd.

R

Long Pond

Pole Rd.

R

R

Y

Snowmobile Trail

P

Flugertown Rd.

Y

Willowemoc Rd.

P

Mongaup Pond

Mongaup Rd.

N

15. MONGAUP/WILLOWEMOC

Intermediate-
Expert

Cross-country
Telemark
Snowshoe

The 8.1-mile trail that leaves Mongaup Pond and arrives at the Black Bear Road trailhead near Round Pond has three trailheads for entering into the trail system. This is a good opportunity to take two cars if you do not want to ski the whole distance. Located in the southwest corner of the Catskill Park, the trail is part of the Willowemoc-Long Pond Wild Forest which contains 14,800 acres of forever-wild forest preserve. The trail is also shared by snowmobilers and may become quite active on weekends, but that will leave a faster track. Mongaup Pond, the largest body of water in the region, is a bustling public campground in the summer and fall, but on cold winter days there may be no one there.

Along a section of the trail is Long Pond, a serene, 15-acre lake with a lean-to located just above its shores, a good spot to break for lunch and bask in the sun. A new trailhead and snowmobile trail, finished in 1997, makes it quicker to ski into Long Pond, though the short trail is more difficult. There are no spectacular mountain views, but there is much primitive wilderness, with meadows and dark forests along the way. The whole length of the trail stays near the 2,000-foot level, so ample snow usually may be found there.

It is advisable to bring a good map for this area. The New York-New Jersey Trail Conference produces perhaps the most detailed map set, called Catskill Trails, for traveling in this region. Looking at map 43 of the series, you will see many communities listed along the roads, but most of them have no stores or gas stations. Traveling from Livingston Manor to Big Indian is an isolated stretch in the winter; prepare well.

Getting There All three trailheads are best approached from Route 17 in the southern Catskills.

For Mongaup Pond: Take Exit 96 on Route 17 at Livingston Manor. At the junction of County Route 179 and County Road 81 (Debruce Road), take County Road 81 which runs northeast under Route 17, passing a motel (after passing the bridge at 2.4 miles, it becomes Sullivan County Route 82). At 5.6 miles look for Sullivan County Route 83 and cross the bridge. At 6.0 miles cross another bridge and make a left onto Mongaup Road; proceed 3.9 miles to the campground parking area.

Black Bear Trailhead: From Claryville (See Appendix A) at intersection of County Roads 19 and 157, turn onto County 157, go over bridge and proceed 1.3 miles to fork in road. Go left uphill on Pond Road (Rough Road) for 0.8 miles; Round Pond will be on the left. Make a right up the hill and proceed 0.2 miles to Black Bear parking area on the right.

Long Pond Trailhead: Located 0.9 miles up Flugertown Road on the right. This is a large parking area.

The Trail Starting at Mongaup Pond parking area, ski over to the southeast area of the pond, enter Loop B and find the snowmobile trail near campsite 38. Follow this trail north to the beginning of the yellow Mongaup-Willowemac Trail. At 2.1 miles, the trail crosses a bridge over Butternut Brook. Following the stream course for a while, the trail swings left. The old woods road at 2.8 miles leads left to private lands. At 3.2 miles the trail joins the Long Pond-Beaverkill Ridge Trail and has both yellow and red markers. This dual-marked section ends at 3.6 miles on Flugertown Road (which will probably be unplowed in winter). Make a right onto the road and glide south for 0.1 miles; look for the red Long Pond-Beaverkill Trail on the left.

The trail rises sharply in sections to the red Long Pond spur trail on the right after 4.1 miles. It is 0.2 miles to the lean-to above the pond. The shoreline of the pond is very spongy and hard to approach in the summer; in winter it is easier to travel along, but keep in mind how far you are from comfort if you should fall into the shallow pond and get wet.

Continuing along the main trail for 5.7 miles will bring you to Basily Road, which is skiable in winter. Make a right onto this road. The last section descends moderately to the Black Bear trailhead after 8.1 miles from Mongaup Pond.

For those who prefer to ski into Long Pond in a short distance, take the snowmobile trail to the left of the bulletin board at the Long Pond parking area on Flugertown Road. The trail crosses a bridge and climbs immediately. The trail levels on the ridge after about 0.5 miles, then descends to the lean-to for a total one-way distance of about 1 mile. Expert skills are required on the return trip, as this is a challenging glide.

16 • Frick Pond

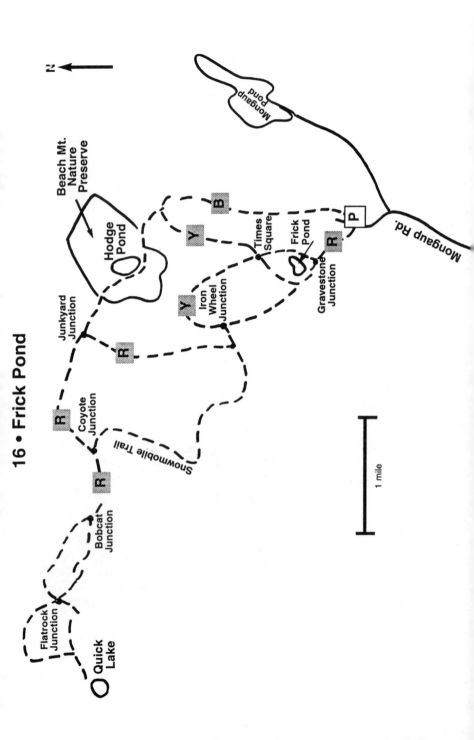

16. FRICK POND

All levels

The Frick Pond region brings the skier to an isolated section of the western Catskills. There is labyrinth of state trails to explore, with several lakes and ponds. This is certainly a classic wilderness traverse, including the all-day 14.4-mile round-trip excursion for the expert skier to Quick Lake. With names like Gravestone Junction and Times Square, the DEC has put a little mystery into the trail system. Many of the trails are old roads that have been seeded with grasses, so the trail bases are particularly well suited for cross-country skiing. The hills and ridges are more rolling and the best views are found in the winter, which can produce some good snows at the trailhead elevation of about 2,000 feet. Several of the trails are also shared by snowmobiles; this may work to the nordic skier's advantage when trying to push heavy new snow. It is also possible to go the entire distance to Quick Lake without seeing or hearing a snowmobile.

Cross-country
Telemark
Snowshoe

Close attention must be given to maps and trail descriptions. A brief description and ability rating is given below for each trail in this area. Note that there are no stores or services available for many miles.

Getting There

Follow directions to Mongaup Pond Campground. Turn north on Mongaup Road and drive 2.7 miles to road fork and make a left onto Beech Mountain Road. (Mongaup campground is 1 mile straight up the road). Proceed 0.4 miles to the double parking area next to Frick Pond trailhead, where there is a DEC bulletin board. Do not continue straight onto private property.

Frick Pond Loop

All Levels

From the rear of the parking lot on left side of road, follow path of the red Quick Lake Trail. (Beginners may have to walk for 0.1 miles but should not get discouraged.) Make a left on the nearly level road (still following red trail markers) to Gravestone Junction at 0.4 miles (grave is on the left.). Continue straight along Quick Trail. At 0.5 miles there is a sudden, steep drop to the pond area, with a large, skiable bridge across the outlet of Frick Pond. Follow Quick Lake Trail from the lake area until it reaches the Big Rock Trail. Make a right, following the yellow markers to Times Square Junction. Make a right onto Loggers Road to complete the loop back to Gravestone Junction.

Quick Lake Trail

Intermediate-Expert

Quick Lake Tail is the longest trail to ski from the Frick Pond Trailhead. There is much gain and loss of elevation on the final 3 miles, so stamina is essential if you are planning to ski the whole route. Looking at a map, you will see the first junction is at Loggers Trail at 0.4 miles, to Frick Pond and Big Rock Trail at 0.7 miles, to Ironwheel Junction at 1.5 miles, to Junkyard Junction at 3.1 miles, and to Quick Lake at 7.2 miles.

Flynn Trail-Hodge Pond Loop

Intermediate-Expert

This attractive, 3.2-mile trail rises over 600 feet during its course and culminates at Junkyard Junction, which makes for several opportunities for the return trip. The Flynn Trail leaves the right (east) side of the road across from the parking area. Follow the blue markers. It is important to avoid side roads and stay on the marked trail. A large meadow is encountered at the edge of Hodge Pond at 2.4 miles. This part of the Beech Mountain Preserve is a private inholding with a New York State easement for foot traffic and nordic skiing. The trail resumes and returns to the state forest preserve before ending at Junkyard Junction.

Big Rock Trail

Expert

From the Flynn Trail, this yellow trail drops steeply to Times Square Junction with a loss of 600 feet in elevation in 1.1 miles. From this junction, the trail changes radically and is level most of the way to the Quick Lake Trail for a total distance of 1.6 miles.

Loggers Trail

Beginner-Intermediate

If you're a novice skier and you feel comfortable for the first 0.4 miles to Frick Pond, continue on. Make a right at Gravestone Junction and cross the open field along the Loggers Trail (Frick Pond should be visible to the left along the way). Times Square is reached after 0.6 miles, and the trail climbs to the its height at 0.8 miles. The trail loops to the west and then to the south to join the Quick Lake Trail at Iron Wheel Junction, named for the iron wheels and axle of an old wagon that are still there.

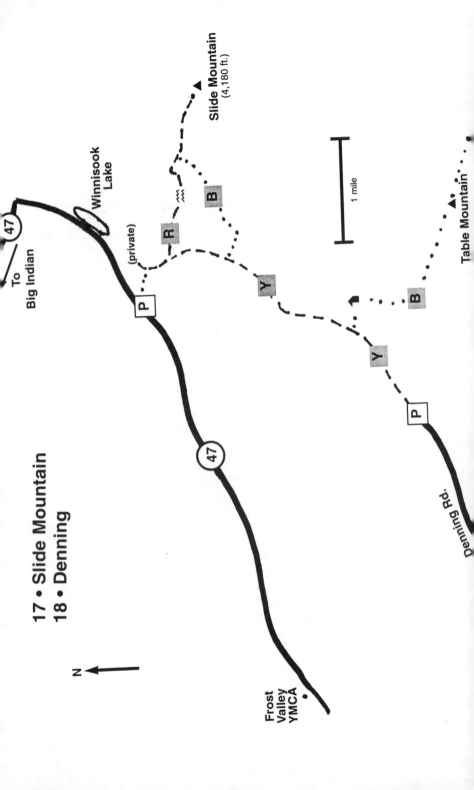

17 • Slide Mountain
18 • Denning

N

To
Big Indian

47

Winnisook
Lake

Slide Mountain
(4,180 ft.)

(private)

R

B

Y

B

Table Mountain

Y

1 mile

P

P

Denning Rd.

47

Frost
Valley
YMCA

17. SLIDE MOUNTAIN

Expert

Telemark
Snowshoe
Snowboard

This guide would be incomplete without some mention of the highest peak in the Catskills: Slide Mountain, which reaches into the sky 4,180 feet, respectable in the Northeast. Like the quarterback in a huddle, Slide is surrounded by big hulks and is not easily viewed at playing-field level. It can be seen from vantage points in the distant Hudson Valley or from the summits of nearby peaks. Because of this, it took a long time for this tallest mountain to be recognized as such; it wasn't until the 1870s that the explorer and professor Arnold Guyot determined that this was indeed the highest of the Catskill peaks. The name Slide was adopted (despite attempts to name it something a bit more grandiose) because of a mammoth rock slide near its summit around 1830.

This is a popular snowshoe hike as this prevents post holing: the deep holes in the snow left by regular hiking with boots. To ski this mountain requires expert skills and, in certain sections on the climb, taking off one's skis and hiking it. Telemark skiing has become more popular here due to the heavy snow pack by late season in a good snow year. It is possible to find 8 feet or more on the top ridge by spring. This makes for fine woods' skiing. Extreme skiers and snowboarders have been known to ski off the north face to Woodland Valley, however, this should only be done expedition style with a group loaded with full survival gear. What is generally a modest climb to the summit with climbing skins may take on a new dimension with severe weather conditions. (See Introduction.) It is best to start early on a mid-winter morning and return well before dusk. Wind-chill factors on the summit ridge may be severe at times; prepare well!

Getting There From NY Route 28 in the hamlet of Big Indian, travel south along County Route 47 toward Claryville. At 7.4 miles there is a hairpin turn, with a parking lot for the trail to Giant Ledge on the right. The road goes steeply uphill to Winnisook Lake at 8.5 miles on the left. This section of road requires four-wheel drive or chains in bad weather. The road then drops moderately downhill; the Slide Mountain parking area is on the left at 9.4 miles. (Frost Valley nordic area is farther on at 14.0 miles.) There is parking for many cars at the Slide trailhead and the parking lot is usually maintained. Prepare well though, as this area is isolated. Alternate: From the south, travel 4.6 miles northeast along County Route 47 from Frost Valley. (See Getting There, page 85.)

The Trail From the parking area, follow the yellow DEC trail markers past the trail board and register. After crossing the West Branch of the Neversink River, it heads east on flat terrain. At 0.2 miles the grade rises steeply (you may want to walk this rock-and-boulder section) to 0.4 miles, where the trail meets an old woods road. Keep right, going left leads to private property. At 0.7 miles, the road reaches the junction of the Slide-Cornell-Wittenburg Trail and the Denning Trail. (See Getting There, page 82.) Turn left and begin the route to the summit.

As the trail base becomes increasingly cobbled and coupled with a more southern exposure, the snow here may not be deep enough to ski, especially in spring. The trail rises rather steeply from 0.5 miles to the 3,500-foot level at 1.1 miles. The deep spring snow pack may be evident at this level, and one can usually ski to the top. The road turns north and then east into the thick balsam forest. In the last 20 years, the road has narrowed considerably as the forest has closed in. Spectacular views are off to the north and northwest.

Looking east:
Wittenberg
and Cornell
from the top
of Slide

At 1.4 miles look for an opening with fine views
south to Table Mountain. The trail reaches the actual
summit at 2.0 miles, but a short ski leads farther to a
meadow overlooking Balsam and Friday Mountains to
the east. Beyond the mountain range are vistas of the
Ashokan Reservoir and the Hudson Valley eventually
to Massachusetts, where on a clear day Mt. Everett
can be seen. A lean-to and fire tower have been re-
moved and the meadow has shrunk considerably since
overnight camping was prohibited. On the base of the
rock shelf there is a memorial to naturalist John Burroughs (1837-1921), whose writings inspired many.
Round trip to the parking area is 5.5 miles.

18. DENNING TRAIL

Intermediate-Expert

Cross-country Telemark Snowshoe

If there is a trail that takes you into the heart and soul of the Catskills, perhaps this is it. Located at 2,100 feet, the trailhead is at the end of a poor road—getting there may be half the adventure. This is the southern approach to Slide Mountain, along an old woods road through some of the most enchanting forest in the region. A mountain pass is reached after 3 miles, where one may want to veer off the trail and snowshoe a southern ridge of Slide Mountain. Statistics show that this area receives the most snowfall in the entire Catskils and a good base of snow usually can be found in spring. This may come in handy, as the upper reaches of the trail have rocky bases in spots. It is also one of the most isolated sections of the Catskills, so its best to go with a group, especially if taking the Curtis-Ormsbee trail. It is also important to keep a wary eye on time and weather in mid-winter. Many of the communities listed on maps are *former* settlements, so plan properly and gas up.

Getting There

From Claryville (see Appendix A) and the intersection of County Route 157 and County Road 19, proceed up County 19 (Denning Road) 8.0 miles northeast to the trailhead parking area. The last several miles of this road are unpaved and in spring may become quite muddy. The parking area is usually maintained and has room for many cars.

The Trails

From the parking lot, sign in at the trail register and go around the barrier gate, following the yellow markers. This first part of the trail is through a hemlock forest and is quite a contrast to the open field by the parking area. The crystalline waters of the East Branch of the Neversink are down on the right. Much of the land is posted along this DEC right-of-way. The old road winds gradually up for 1.2 miles, crossing over several brooks and occasional forest openings until the intersection with the blue trail on the right. This hiking trail leads to a lean-to at 0.3 miles. Beyond that are the summits of Table and Peekamoose Mountains, both rising over 3,800 feet. To climb them would require snowshoes; many parts are quite steep.

Wild turkeys near the Denning trailhead.

The yellow trail continues up gradual grades to the height of the land, where more expert skills are required. At this elevation—3,050 feet—you have ascended 1,000 feet above the trailhead in over 3 miles. The intermediate skier may want to return from this junction. Those continuing will find the blue-marked Curtis-Ormsbee trail on the right. (The designers of the trail, William Curtis and Allen Ormsbee, both perished in 1900, as have many others, in the unpredictable, fearsome weather of Mount Washington in New Hampshire. A small stone monument to Curtis is at this trail junction, although it may go unnoticed in deep snow.) This is the least-traveled trail to the sum-

83

mit of Slide, and it offers some fine views along the 1.6-mile route. Expert skills are required because there are several short rises over large rocks; these sections require some climbing and maneuvering. Use crampons and extreme caution in icy conditions. Snowshoes are needed in other sections.

Just past the 3,500-foot elevation sign on the blue trail, an impressive view south to Table, Peekamoose, and Lone Mountains can be had from a ledge known as Paul's Lookout. It also gives a perspective of the East Branch of the Neversink valley you have just skied. Soon after, the trail levels for a good distance through a spellbinding forest on the ridge before rising sharply once more. It joins the red Slide-Cornell Trail, which rises gradually 0.7 miles, right to the summit of Slide. A left brings you back over some expert terrain for 1.3 miles to the yellow Denning Trail (see Slide Mountain). At this junction it is 3.8 miles back to the Denning trailhead.

High on the Curtis-Ormsbee Trail

19. FROST VALLEY

All Levels

Fee

Recommended
for Children

Cross-country
Snowshoe

There is a 4,900-acre YMCA environmental education facility located just southeast of Slide Mountain that provides superb nordic skiing for the whole family, with overnight accommodations and hearty meals available. Located at the 2,000-foot level, this valley on the southern fringe of the Catskills offers abundant snow over a long season and should be investigated when snow is not present elsewhere in the Catskills. There are more than 35 kilometers of trails, including 10 kilometers track set. Ski rentals are in the barn area next to the road. Most important to the beginner is the availability of group instruction.

Getting There

From Exit 16 at Harriman on the Thruway, travel west on NY Route 17 to Exit 100 at Liberty. At end of the ramp, make a left and go to the first traffic light, then make a left on to Route 52 west. Go 1 mile and make a sharp right on to Route 55 east. Travel 10 miles to Curry; look for a sign for Claryville on the right and make a left on to County Route 19 and travel 4.0 miles to Claryville. At the sign for Frost Valley on the right, turn left on to County Route 157 and proceed 7.0 miles to Frost Valley.

Alternate: From NY Route 28 and County Route 47 in Big Indian, travel south toward Claryville 14.0 miles to Frost Valley. This route is not recommended in bad weather due to a steep mountain pass.

The Trails

There are a diverse trails from which to choose. A trail map is available in the rental/instruction area to help you make your choice. Beginners can enjoy the flat field area with the large castle looming above it. At the end of the east field area is a wire bridge over the

West Branch of the Neversink River, which makes for a good exercise in balance. Some of the trails reach 500 feet higher than the valley below and nice views can be expected. Several trails behind Thomas Hall reach deep into the hollows of Doubletop Mountain. At 3,860 feet, it is the eighth-highest peak in the Catskills, although it does not seem so from this base altitude.

More info. There is a trail fee, and lunch is available. The nearest general store is located 7 miles away in Claryville. For more information, call (845)985-2291.

20. KENNETH L. WILSON STATE PARK

**Beginner-
Intermediate**

**Recommended
for Children**

**Cross-country
Snowshoe**

Nestled in a photogenic valley, this large state park is located in the hamlet of Wittenburg, part of the township of Woodstock. Large meadows, thick stands of pine, and extensive wetlands characterize its terrain. Situated at 1,000 feet, the park offers impressive views of the Cornell and Wittenburg peaks towering to the west. In the summer there is a fee for use of the lake and campgrounds, but there is no toll in winter, and there are usually no crowds. Much of the area is flat, making it ideal for children, but there are no provisions or restrooms in the wintertime.

Getting There

From NY Route 28 at the school in Boiceville, travel 2.2 miles west toward Phoenicia and make a right onto NY Route 212. Proceed 0.5 miles, then make a sharp right at the intersection onto Wittenburg Road (County Route 40). Travel 3.8 miles to the park entrance on the right. Drive the short distance to the parking area by the lake (there is room for many cars in the well-maintained lot).

Alternate: From the village green in Woodstock, travel 2.0 miles west to Bearsville on Route 212. Keep left over the bridge going up Wittenburg Road County Route 40 (Wittenburg Road). Park entrance is 4.3 miles on the left.

The Trail

There is much open expanse near the parking area, so many people freelance in this vicinity. Skiing on the lake is potentially dangerous, so stick to the shoreline, even in frigid weather. The barrier gate by the bathhouse is the most popular point to start to ski. Traveling west along the road will bring you to the campsite loops. Loop C has some designated winter hiking trail

20 • WILSON STATE PARK

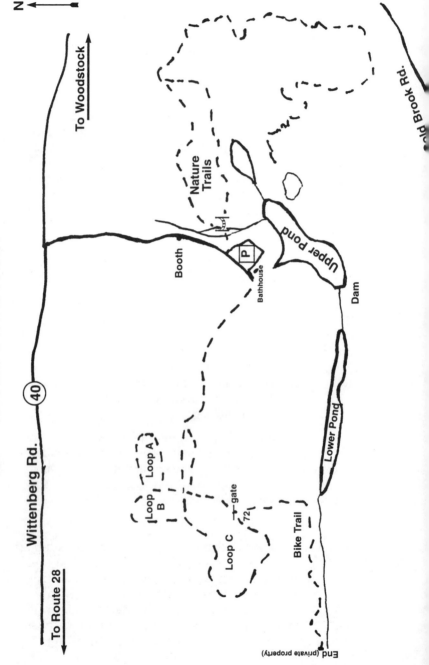

markers in yellow. At camp marker 72, there is another barrier gate with a bike trail marker. This leads you to the lower pond area and follows the stream outlet.

At the east side of the parking area, opposite the bathhouse, a small bridge marks the beginning of a new trail into the thick pine-and-hemlock forest. In cold weather, the open meadows are susceptible to the strong northwest winds which funnel through the valley, and you may want to seek relief in the sheltered campground area.

After a good outing you may decide to travel to nearby Woodstock. You won't find any festival site here; the shindig in 1969 was held in Bethel, 60 miles away, and the one in 1994 was held in Saugerties, 10 miles to the east. However, there are several excellent restaurants and unique shops in which to browse.

21 • Kanape

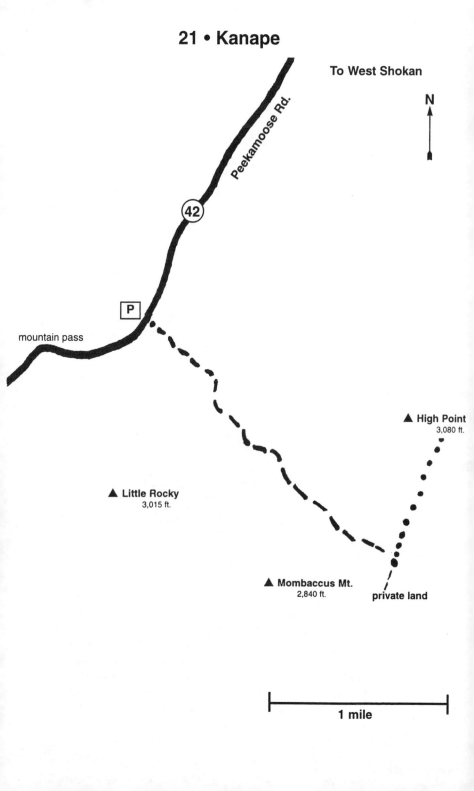

To West Shokan

N

Peekamoose Rd.

42

P

mountain pass

▲ High Point
3,080 ft.

▲ Little Rocky
3,015 ft.

▲ Mombaccus Mt.
2,840 ft.

private land

1 mile

21. KANAPE

Intermediate-
Expert

Cross-country
Telemark
Snowshoe

One of the most popular spots for a panoramic view of the Catskills is from the dike area of the Ashokan Reservoir. This body of water is the largest in New York City's expansive water system. There are two basins of slightly different elevations, with a long wall and bridge between them known as the dividing weir. Looking to the southwest from here one sees majestic High Point, rising 2,500 feet above the upper basin to a summit of 3,080 feet. Hidden behind its southwest side is the Kanape Trail, which follows an old carriage road along a bubbling stream that feeds into the Ashokan. This unmarked DEC trail leads deep into a hollow, rising to a col between High Point and Mombaccus Mountain. The trail base is in reasonably good condition. From this point it is best to hike or snowshoe to the summit of High Point because of the abrupt climb.

Getting There

From NY Routes 28 and 28A in Boiceville, proceed over bridge 3 miles on 28A and make right on County Road 42 (Peekamoose Road) in West Shokan. Travel 4.1 miles to DEC parking area on the right, where there is room for several cars. The trailhead is across the road, 100 yards back. There are many stores in nearby Boiceville.

The Trail

The trail begins at the barrier gate at the 1,100-foot level and crosses a brown wooden bridge across the Kanape Brook. With the brook to the right, the woods road rises through a hardwood forest. Stone walls in the woods indicate past clearings and farms dating to the late 1800s. After 0.6 miles of low, intermediate terrain, the trail crosses an old stone bridge, then another one at 1.5 miles. Shortly after, the brook turns

away from the trail to the north. The trail rises moderately to the col (the height of the road after 2.7 miles is 2,050 feet); the skiing portion ends here. In winter, there are views through the woods to the southeast. The road descends onto private property ahead. The trail turns left, as indicated by the DEC sign. This is the southern, exposed side of the mountain and snow depths may be considerably less. Hiking or snowshoeing the rest of the 1-mile distance to the summit may be a possibility. The summit is not cleared; no large hotel was ever constructed there, although one was considered in the late 1800s because of its dramatic views.

22. SKI PLATTEKILL

Intermediate-Expert

This older, traditional Catskill ski area has long been favored by powder enthusiasts and extreme-skiing buffs. Built in the days before snowmaking, the area is located high on the side of the mountain. There are many miles of mountain biking trails that can double for cross-country, telemark, and snowshoe trails. For a small fee, the winter hiker can quickly ascend on the chairlift to the top ridge of over 3,300 feet, where deeper snows may be found. The only way down is over specially marked trails down a 1,000-foot vertical. A great view of the Catskills lies to the east.

Cross-country
Telemark
Snowshoe
Downhill
Snow tubing

Getting There

From the south on NY Route 28 in Arkville: Turn north on the road near the railroad tracks. There is a sign for Ski Plattekill on the east side of a farm machinery building there. Go 1 mile to NY Route 30. Make a right and proceed for 6.5 miles. Watch for the Ski Plattekill sign; make a left and follow signs to the ski area.

From the north at the intersection of NY Routes 23 and 30 in Grand Gorge: Take 30 south 7 miles to Roxbury. From Roxbury: follow signs.

More info.

For more information: 1-800-NEED-2-SKI or (607) 326-3500, www.plattekill.com. Call for rental information

The ice monsters of Slide Mountain. Heavy cloud cover can leave a foot or more of rime ice on trees on summits. This phenomenon is best observed in late winter or early spring.

Eastern _____

23. ONTEORA LAKE

**Beginner-
Intermediate**

**Cross-country
Snowshoe**

Beer discount, deli, bakery, restaurant, wine shop—all
the amenities are right at the beginning of the Onteora
Lake Trail. Formerly the site of a summer retreat and
trailer park, the trail that surrounds the lake offers diverse forest and wetlands just off the NY Route 28
corridor, within minutes of Kingston. Because the lake
is located below Route 28, the sounds of nearby traffic are lost and it is remarkably quiet when skiing here.
Beginner skiers will be fine on the level area next to
the lake; there are a few difficult spots along the trail
around the lake.

Nestled in the foothills of the Catskills, the lake
has the lowest elevation of the trailheads. As there
are numerous springs along the route, it may be advisable to ski here in weather cold enough to keep the
trail base frozen solid. Although most of the trail is
grassy, a few sections have rocks, so a snow base of
a foot or more is recommended.

Getting There

From Exit 19 of the Thruway at Kingston: Go west
from the traffic circle on NY Route 28 toward Pine
Hill. Proceed 4.1 miles and make right on the dirt road
immediately the before shopping area. Park by the barrier gate with the DEC sign. If plowed, there is room
for several cars.

The Trail

From barrier gate on NY Route 28, glide gently down
the road (if it's not plowed) 0.3 miles to the bulletin
board and parking area. An old woods road around the
lake begins here and parallels the shoreline for 0.2

95

23 • Onteora Lake

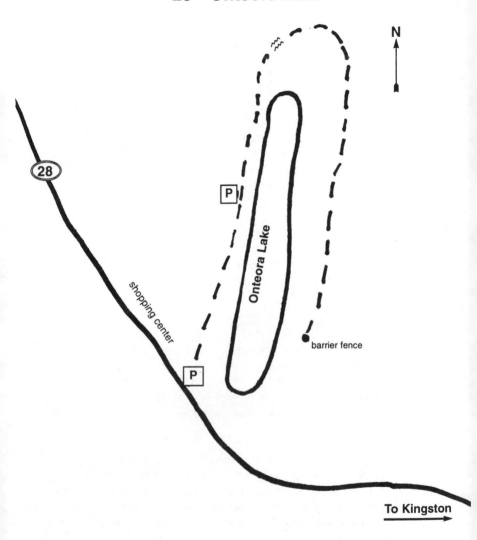

28

shopping center

Onteora Lake

P

P

barrier fence

N

To Kingston

¼ mile

miles to the northeast where it enters the deciduous forest. (Beginners may want to end here; there are several short rises and drops along the trail.) The most significant challenge is at 0.6 miles, where there is a steep drop and a small rock ledge, which may be better to sidestep or walk around. Keep to the right, following the contour of the lake (although you will probably not see it).

The trail enters a hemlock forest; there are several old paths and wood roads to the left to explore, but just make sure to respect private lands. After passing several rises and dips that require some careful negotiating, the trail reaches the height of the land at a barrier fence marking the end of state land. There is talk of continuing the trail farther on to Route 28, but for now this is the turnaround. The glide back is refreshing. Total roundtrip from Route 28 is 4 miles.

24. WILLIAMS LAKE RESORT

All Levels

Trail Fee

Recommended for Children

Cross-country

Not quite in the Catskills, not quite in the Shawan-gunks, but quite an interesting place to cross-country ski, charming Williams Lake is located just 10 minutes from Kingston. The hotel is situated on 600 acres of woodlands and offers over 10 kilometers of groomed and another 10 kilometers of marked (but not groomed) trails. The hotel overlooks a 40-acre, spring-fed lake, and it has become a popular spot for over-night and day-use skiers. A ski shop offers rental equipment and instruction.

Getting There

From Exit 18 of the NYS Thruway at New Paltz, drive west on Route 299 through New Paltz and make right on NY Route 32 north. Proceed 7 miles to Rosendale and make left just over the bridge onto NY Route 213. Go through the village and make right on Binnewater Road; follow signs for Williams Lake Hotel.

More info.

For travel directions and more information, call (845)658-3101 or 1-800-382-3818 or write Williams Lake Hotel, P.O. Box 474, Rosendale, NY 12472

Shawangunks

One of the best vantage points to view the Catskills is from the nearest mountain range, the Shawangunks. Only 10 miles from in the southeast Catskills, the Shawangunks are geologically distinct from the Catskills, which are composed mainly of sedimentary rock formations. The Shawangunk Ridge extends south from the Kingston area, rising to its highest point of 2,289 feet at Sam's Point, between Ellenville and New Paltz. The ridge extends all the way to Pennsylvania. The unique rock formations consist of quartz conglomerate. Many white cliffs can be easily seen in the area, which is world famous for rock climbing. Because of the hard rock surfaces, the soil is poor and the area supports its own unusual ecosystem, including pitch pine and dwarf pitch pine stands, some of which are more than 300 years old.

The "Gunks," as they are referred to by rock climbers, are also home to several deep, clear lakes near the top of the ridges. Lake Mohonk and Lake Minnewaska both are accessible to the nordic skier.

**Lake
Minnewaska**

Built in 1879 with additions in 1888, 1893, 1899, 1902 and 1910, Lake Mohonk Mountain House is a Victorian treasure and was designated a National Historic Landmark in 1986.

25. LAKE MOHONK MOUNTAIN HOUSE

All Levels

Admission Fee

Cross-country

Lake Mohonk and the surrounding Mohonk Mountain House property offer many miles of cross-country skiing along old carriage roads and groomed paths. Inspired by the stunning landscape on an outing in 1869, twin brothers Alfred and Albert Smiley set out to create one of the most picturesque hotels in the world. Originally used as a summer retreat, the hotel was gradually winterized starting in 1933 when winter sports began gaining popularity. Lake Mohonk sits at an elevation of 1,247 feet; it is a half-mile long and up to 60 feet deep. The sprawling Mohonk Mountain House towers over the lake like a Victorian castle. One of the few great resorts left from the nineteenth century, it is designated a National Historic Landmark. Day visitors may use the hotel's nordic facilities during the weekdays; rentals are available. There is an admission fee.

Getting There

More info.

See chapter 26, Mohonk Preserve, for directions. Note that the Mohonk Preserve and the Mohonk Mountain House are separate entities. For more information, call (845)255-1000, or write Mohonk Mountain House, Lake Mohonk, New Paltz, New York 12561.

26. MOHONK PRESERVE

All Levels

Admission Fee

Recommended for Children

Cross-country
Snowshoe
Rock Climbing

The largest member- and visitor-supported nature pre-serve in New York State, the Mohonk Preserve offers visitors access to 6,400 acres—including cliffs, for-ests, fields, ponds, streams—and to more than 100 miles of carriage roads and trails for hiking, cross-coun-try skiing and snowshoeing. Visitors are welcome seven days a week on Preserve lands and at The Trapps Gateway Visitors' Center, which features ex-hibits, a "Kids' Corner" discovery area, self-guiding trails, and a nature shop. Admission to the Visitors' Center is free. Preserve lands are open sunrise to sun-set, and a current membership or day-entry pass is re-quired. Rent equipment in town at Peak Performance or Rock & Snow; there are no rentals on site. The tails are sometimes groomed.

Getting There

Directions to the Visitors' Center from the New York State Thruway: Leave the Thruway at Exit 18 (New Paltz). At the traffic light, turn left onto NY Route 299 West. Continue on 299 through New Paltz and across the Wallkill River for 6 miles to the T-junction with NY Routes 44/55. Turn right at the stop sign onto 44/55. The Visitors' Center entrance is 1/2 mile on the right. Turn into the first parking lot.

More Info:

More information: Consult www.mohonkpreserve.org for travel directions, trail recommendations, current weather, and other visitor information. For daily trail conditions, call the Preserve at (845) 255-0919.

27. MINNEWASKA STATE PARK PRESERVE

All Levels

Trail Fee

Recommended for Children

Cross-country
Snowshoe

Several miles over along the Shawangunk Ridge is Lake Minnewaska, located in the Minnewaska State Park Preserve. Viewing the lake in any season is inspiring. When not frozen over, the water is turquoise—truly unique for the Northeast. Lake Minnewaska had two large hotels above the cliffs surrounding it until the 1980s when both were destroyed by fires. Efforts to commercialize the mountaintop were halted, and this treasured area became a state park operated by the Palisades Interstate Park Commission.

Much of the park is at 2,000 feet, and ample snow may be found here. There are 26 miles of trails, some groomed and/or marked, leading to views from along the ridge of the agricultural landscape and surrounding towns and villages in the valley below. Other trails lead for several miles to Lake Awosting, another dazzling Shawangunk lake. The park preserve is a very popular cross-country ski destination, with many services offered such as ski rentals, lessons and services for larger groups.

Getting There

From Exit 18 on the Thruway at New Paltz, motor west though New Paltz on Route 299 approximately 7.5 miles to Route 44/55. Proceed right on 44/55 west toward Kerhonskon for 4 miles; look for the park entrance on the left.

More info.

Call (845)255-0752, or write Minnewaska State Park Preserve, P.O. Box 893, New Paltz, NY. 12561

APPENDIX A: Claryville Route Guide

To reach Claryville from Route 28 or from the north, begin at the intersection of NY Route 28 and County Road 47 in the hamlet of Big Indian (by the general store). Proceed 19.6 miles up County Road 47 over the steep mountain pass at Slide Mountain to the junction of County Routes 47 and 157. Follow signs to Claryville on County Route 157. At 20.9 miles cross the bridge over the Neversink River and make a left on County Road 19 to go to the post office and general store.

From the south or NY Route 17 corridor, take Exit 100 off Route 17 at Liberty. At the exit make a left at the first traffic light, then go left again onto Route 52 west. After 1 mile make a sharp right on Route 55 east. Proceed 10 miles to Curry and look for a sign on right for Claryville. Turn left onto County Road 19 and travel over the mountain 4 miles to Claryville.

APPENDIX B: Other Nordic Ski Possibilities

BEAR PEN MOUNTAIN

Intermediate-Expert
Cross-country
Telemark
Snowshoe

This is on the site of an old Catskill Ski area. The trail follows an old woods road through Bear Pen Mountain State Forest 4 miles on a right-of-way to a summit of over 3,600 feet. There are one or two difficult sections which are good for a telemark climb using skins. The top ridge is flat for miles so cross-country in con-

Opposite page: Norway spruce forest in Kelly Hollow (chap. 14).

juntion with snowshoes is all right, too. The trail is frequently used by snowmobiles. Loggers may rip up the bottom mile or so early in the season before the heavy snows set in.

Getting There From NY Route 23 and the Schoharie Creek Bridge in Prattsville: Turn onto County Route 2 and proceed up a long hill. After 2.5 miles, Harry Peckham Road is on the left. At 2.6 miles Bearpen Mountain is straight in front of you across the valley. At 2.7 miles on the right is a street sign for Ski Run Road. Park carefully off the road as there is no DEC parking area.

PEEKAMOOSE-BULL RUN

Beginner-Intermediate

Cross-country Snowshoe

Located at the outlet of a deep gorge, this campground meadow offers easy skiing and snowshoeing on the site of an early settlement. Getting there is half the fun as the road from West Shokan has many waterfalls, and in the winter, they take on a magic of their own. These are the headwaters of Rondout Creek.

Getting There From the junction of NY Route 28 and County Route 42 (Peekamoose Road) in West Shokan: Travel west on County Route 42 toward Sundown. At 3.9 miles the Kanape Trail is on the left. From here the road goes over a mountain pass. Look for Buttermilk falls at 8.5 miles. A 11.6 miles look for the DEC parking area on the right for Bull Run. Follow the trail from the parking area to the fields below. From the south at Grahamsville: Go east on NYS Route 55 a short distance and make a left on 55A. When 55A makes a sharp turn to the right, go straight on County Route 153 (the number changes to 46 when you cross into Ulster County just before Sundown). At Sundown bear left on Route 42to Bull Run.

APPENDIX C: Catskill Downhill Ski Areas

BELLEAYRE MOUNTAIN SKI CENTER: Downhill, snowboarding, cross-country, rentals, instruction

34 miles west of Kinston off NY Route 28 in Highmount, Ulster County. Snow Phone: 800-942-6904. Tel.: 845-254-5600. 1404' vert. drop, 35 trails, max. length: 2.27 miles, 92% snowmaking. www.belleayre.com

BOBCAT: Downhill, snowboarding, rentals, instruction

2.5 miles off NY Route 28 in Andes, Delaware County. Snow phone: 845-676-3143, Tel.: 845-676-3143. 1050 vert. drop, 19 trails, max. length: 1.5 mi.), 20% snowmaking.

HOLIDAY MOUNTAIN: Downhill, snowboarding, snow tubing, snowshoeing, rentals, instruction

Exit 19 on NY Route 17 (I-86) near Monticello, Sullivan County. Tel.: 845-796-3161. 400' vert. drop, 15 trails, max. length: .92 mi., 100% snowmaking. www.holidaymtn.com

HUNTER MOUNTAIN: Downhill, snowboarding, snow tubing, snowshoeing, rentals, instruction

In the village of Hunter on NY Route 23A, Greene County, Snow phone: 800-FOR-SNOW. Tel.: 518-263-4223. 1600' vert. drop, 53 trails, max. length: 2 mi., 100% snowmaking. www.huntermtn.com

KUTSHER'S COUNTRY CLUB: Downhill, cross-country, snowboarding, snowshoeing, toboganning, ice skating, rentals, instruction

Exit 105B on NY Route 17, 1st light left on Anawana Lake Rd. 3 mi, Sullivan County. Tel.: 800-431-1273. 150' vert. drop, 2 trails, max. length: 500 ft., 100% snowmaking. www.kutshers.com

SAWKILL FAMILY SKI CENTER: Downhill, snowbarding, snow tubing, instruction.

Exit 19 (Kingston) on NYS Thruway, take the first right one-half mile to NY Route 209 North. Go 2 miles to the Sawkill exit. Turn left at the bottom of the ramp on Sawkill Road (following green ski signs) for 2-1/2 miles. Turn left on Jockey Hill Road and go up the hill 1 mile. Turn left on Hill Road and go one-third mile to the parking lot. Snowmaking. www.sawkillski.com

SKI PLATTEKILL MOUNTAIN RESORT: Downhill, cross-country, snowtubing, snowboarding, rentals, intstruction.

[Directions: see page 94] 1000' vert. drop, 32 trails, max. length: 2 mi., 75% snowmaking. www.plattekill.com

SKI WINDHAM: Downhill, snow tubing, snowboarding, snowshoeing, rentals, instruction

Exit 21 on NYS Thruway, NY Route 23 to Windham, Greene County. Tel.: 800-SKI-WINDHAM. 1600' vert. drop. 34 trails, max. length: 2.3 mi., 97% snowmaking. www.enjoyhv.com

VILLA ROMA: Downhill, snow tubing, snowboarding, toboganning, rentals, instruction

Exit 104 on NY Route 17 (I-86) to 17B West for 17 mi., follow signs, Sullivan County. Tel.: 800-727-8455. 250' vert. drop, 5 trails, max. length: .25 mi. 100% snowmaking. www.villaroma.com

APPENDIX D: NYSDEC Regional Offices

Region 3 Headquarters, 21 South Putt Rd., New Paltz, NY 12561, (845)256-3000

Region 4 District Office, Jefferson Rd., Stamford, NY 12167, (607)652-7365

APPENDIX E: Useful Publications and Maps

Catskill Center for Conservation and Development. The Catskills (road map), 2nd edition. Arkville, NY, 1986

DeLisser, Richard Lionel. *Picturesque Catskills: Greene County*. Reprinted by Hope Farm Press, Cornwallville, NY, 1967. *Picturesque Ulster*. Reprinted by Hope Farm Press, Saugerties, NY, 1998.

Dunn, John M., M.D. *Winterwize: A Backpacker's Guide*. Adirondack Mountain Club, Lake George, NY, 1996

Evers, Alf. *The Catskills: From Wilderness to Woodstock*. Doubleday, Garden City, NY, 1972. Reprinted by The Overlook Press, Woodstock, NY, 1982.

Henry, Edward G. *Catskill Trails: A Ranger's Guide to the High Peaks*, 2 vols., Black Dome Press, Hensonville, NY, 2000.

Horne, Field. *The Greene County Catskills: A History*. Black Dome Press, Hensonville, NY, 1994.

Jimapco. County road maps for Greene, Ulster, Delaware and Sullivan Counties.

McAllister and Ochman. *Hiking the Catskills*. New York-New Jersey Trail Conference, New York, NY, 1995.

Podskoch, Martin, *Fire Towers of the Catskills*. Purple Mountain Press, Fleischmanns, NY, 2000.

New York-New Jersey Trail Conference. Catskill Trails. 7th edition of a five-map set, 2001.

Thaler, Jerome. *Catskill Weather*. Purple Mountain Press, Fleischmanns, NY, 1996.

Titus, Robert. *The Catskills: A Geological Guide.* Purple Mountain Press, Fleischmanns, NY, rev.ed., 1998.

Titus, Robert. *The Catskills: In the Ice Age.* Purple Mountain Press, Fleischmanns, New York, 1996.

Wadsworth, Bruce. *A Guide to Catskill Trails.* Adirondack Mountain Club, Lake George, NY, 1994.

Index

Acknowledgments

I would like to thank the following people for their help and inspiration for the creation of this book. Hiking companions: Jim Weider, Arthur Smith, Wolf Carl, Gail Stopczynski, Jim Curtain, Bernadette Quinn, Janine Bourden, Osku Backstrom, Howard Rifken, and all the state forest rangers. Cover photos: David Carlson.

In wilderness is the preservation of the world.
Henry David Thoreau

Purple Mountain Press, Ltd., established 1973, is a publishing company committed to producing the best new books of regional and maritime interest and bringing back into print significant older works. Of special interest to readers of this book will be our *The Catskills: A Bicycling Guide* by Pierre Menetrier and Jay Wenk and *Catskill Weather* by Jerome Thaler. For a free catalog of more than 300 books about the Catskills and New York State, write Purple Mountain Press, Ltd., P.O. Box 309, Fleischmanns, NY 12430, or call 845-254-4062, or fax 845-254-4476, or email purple@catskill.net. Visit our website at http://www.catskill.net/purple.